Boeing
Boeing's First Jetliner

RON MAK

HISTORIC COMMERCIAL AIRCRAFT SERIES, VOLUME 2

Front cover image: PH-TVA, Boeing 707-123 of Transavia Holland, at Schiphol Airport, Amsterdam, in May 1981.

Back cover image: HC-BDP, a special-liveried Boeing 720-023B of Ecuatoriana (Ecuador), at Mariscal Sucre International Airport, Quito, on 28 October 1977.

Title page image: EL-ZGS *Maritza*, Boeing 707-309C of Jet Cargo-Liberia, at Sharjah Airport, United Arab Emirates, in 1995.

Published by Key Books
An imprint of Key Publishing Ltd
PO Box 100
Stamford
Lincs PE19 1XQ

www.keypublishing.com

The right of Ron Mak to be identified as the author of this book has been asserted in accordance with the Copyright, Designs and Patents Act 1988 Sections 77 and 78.

Copyright © Ron Mak, 2021

ISBN 978 1 913870 89 8

All photographs copyright of the author unless otherwise stated

Typeset by SJmagic DESIGN SERVICES, India.

Introduction

Between 1949 and 1950, Boeing concentrated its future transport studies on advanced jet and turboprop versions of the model 377 Stratocruiser, which had been developed from the C-97 Stratofreighter military transport (itself derived from the B-29 Superfortress), and a few C-97s were flown with turboprop engines. However, the success of the de Havilland Comet gradually convinced Boeing that jet power was the way forward, along with a design much more advanced than any improved Stratocruiser. Studies were given the same '367' Boeing model number as the C-97, though they increasingly departed from the Stratofreighter's shape.

By late 1951, all the 367-series studies were centred around the use of four Pratt & Whitney JT3 turbojets, the civil version of the J57 engine used in the company's B-52 heavy bomber. Neither the B-52 nor the earlier B-47 airframes were suitable as the basis for a jetliner, and a series of studies, designated 367-40 to 367-80, continued searching for the best arrangement of wing, engines and landing gear. The one consistent feature was the fuselage cross-section, larger than that of the C-97, and with the sides of the C-97's 'double bubble' filled in to give an approximately oval form.

In early 1952, it was decided that the 367-80 configuration was the optimum achievable at that time. The wing was swept back at 35° and had a thick root that filled the space under the cabin floor where the spar box crossed the fuselage. The engines were housed in separate widely spaced pods, hung well forward and below the wing, and the aircraft rested on two, four-wheel main undercarriage units that retracted inwards from pivots on the wing to occupy large bays in the fuselage, plus a twin nosewheel unit that retracted forwards. After further discussions with the United States Air Force (the finished design would be used for a variety of military roles), Boeing secured acceptance of the design in principle but chose to manage and finance the programme itself.

On 20 May 1952, Boeing president Bill Allen announced the decision to build the prototype. At a cost of more than $20 million, it was at that time the largest risk ever accepted by an aircraft manufacturer.

In July 1955, the United States Air Force had formally given consent to sales of a civil version of the aircraft, enabling Boeing to use the same tooling for the military (predominantly KC-135 air-to-air refuelling tankers) and civil types. The civil version of the new aircraft was now designated Boeing 707. By the late 1950s, the demand for both civil and military variants was so high that the tooling had to be expensively multiplied to increase the total output to as many as 35 aircraft a month.

At first, the production of civil Boeing 707s was modest, and the first Boeing 707-121 – built for Pan American World Airways – did not fly until 20 December 1957. Observers noticed its long row of small passenger windows, two for each seat row on each side of the fuselage, contrasting with the larger windows of rival airliners. Pan American inaugurated 707 passenger services on 26 October 1958, and although the 707-121 was intended for domestic operations, Pan Am used it initially on its New York-to-Paris transatlantic route, with a stopover in Newfoundland.

A shorter-range version of the 707 was developed to fly from shorter runways, featuring a 9ft (2.7m)-shorter fuselage, a modified wing and lightened airframe, and christened the Boeing 720. This variant could carry 156 passengers and first flew in November 1959, entering service in July 1960. One hundred and fifty four Boeing 720 variants were built in total.

Production of civil 707s would continue until 1978, with production of military models continuing until 1991. More than 1,000 Boeing 707 variants were built in total, operated by airlines and air forces around the world. The final 707s in civilian service were operated by Iran's Saha Air, which ceased operation of the type in 2014, more than 55 years after the 707 first entered passenger service with Pan Am. Arguably, the Boeing 707 created the template for worldwide air travel today.

Ron Mak
Almere, Netherlands, April 2021

PH-TRF, Boeing 707-355C of Transavia Holland, pictured at Schiphol Airport, Amsterdam, on 25 November 1968. This aircraft was delivered to Executive Jet Aviation on 9 November 1967 as N526EJ. It was then leased to Transavia Holland from 15 May 1968 to 14 October 1969, as PH-TRF. Transavia Holland, known as Transavia until 1967, was founded in 1965 and began charter and inclusive-tour operations on 17 November 1966. The initial fleet consisted of Douglas DC-6Bs , but these were soon replaced by more-modern jets – SE.210 Caravelles, Boeing 707s and Boeing 737s. On 8 August 1967, this 707 left for a cargo flight to Central African island São Tomé with a 30-ton cargo of baby milk for the children in Biafra. At that time, the 707 was the largest aircraft to land at São Tomé.

N70700, the Boeing 367-80 prototype, seen in November 1978 in storage at the Military Aircraft Storage and Disposition Center (MASDC), located at Davis-Monthan AFB, Arizona. The grey, chocolate-brown and yellow prototype of the new airliner was rolled out of the assembly hangar at Boeing's Renton plant, Washington state, on 15 May 1954. Though many continued to refer to it as the 367-80, or more simply as the 'Dash 80', this aircraft was publicised as the Boeing Model 707, and it was no coincidence that it was registered as N70700. This 707 was intended solely as an experimental aircraft to test the new configuration, and was never fitted out to carry passengers.

N707PA, Pan American World Airways Boeing 707-121, at Mexico City Airport on 5 November 1971. The first Boeing 707-100-series aircraft, equipped with Pratt & Whitney JT3C-6 engines, made its first flight on 20 December 1957, and such was the momentum of the production effort, that the first example was delivered to Pan American World Airways in August 1958. Pan American placed an order for eight B707-120s, which were delivered between 1958 and 1962. This photograph shows the author about to board a flight from Mexico City to Miami in 1971 – his first 707 flight. Today, 50 years later, including this photograph in a book about the Boeing 707 brings back happy memories. N707PA was the second 707 to leave the production line.

N707PA, Pan American World Airways' *Clipper Maria*, a Boeing 707-121, at Idlewind Airport, New York (later renamed John F Kennedy International Airport) on 23 April 1966. This was the second Boeing 707-121 to leave the production line. Delivered to Pan American on 19 December 1958, this aircraft was leased to Pan Ayer in March 1974, then sub-leased to Turkish Airlines as TC-JBA until February 1975, returning to Pan Ayer as HP-780. It resumed its original identity as N707PA in August 1979, and was bought by International Air Leases in November 1983. The aircraft was broken up at Miami International Airport in May 1988.

TC-JBD, Turkish Airlines Boeing 707-121, at Istanbul Airport, Yesilköy, on 20 April 1974. Delivered to Pan American as N712PA *Clipper Washington* in October 1958, this 707 was leased to Pan Ayer in February 1974, then sub-leased to Turkish Airlines from February 1974 to May 1976 as TC-JBD. It was later leased to Bouraq Airlines (Indonesia) and Air Asia, and finally broken up at Taipei Airport, Taiwan, in August 1984.

9M-AQD, a Boeing 707-321 of Southern Cross Airways (Malaysia), at Stansted Airport on 27 December 1971. A short-lived airline, Southern Cross Airways operated from 1971 to 1972 with regular flights from Kuala Lumpur to London Gatwick, although the aircraft was also seen at the Pan American maintenance area at London Heathrow. Delivered to Pan American as N714PA in August 1958, the aircraft was bought by Southern Cross in June 1971, before being repossessed by Pan Am in June 1972. It then went to Miami for storage and was later sold to Perfect Air Tours, as N714PT, prior to being broken up at Boeing Field, Seattle, in August 1981.

TC-JAH *Bergama*, Turkish Airlines Boeing 707-321, seen at Schiphol Airport, Amsterdam, on 21 March 1971. Delivered to Pan American World Airways in July 1959 as N715PA *Clipper Liberty Bell*, this aircraft was leased to Turkish Airlines from January 1971 to January 1974, then bought by lease operator Tempair International Airlines as 9G-ACB. It was leased to DETA (Mozambique Airlines) as C9-ARF in March 1976.

C9-ARF, a Boeing 707-321 of DETA (Mozambique Airlines), at Brussels Airport, Zaventem, on 17 February 1977. Mozambique gained independence from Portugal in 1975, and international airline services started in 1976, serving the Lourenço Marques–Beira–Accra–Lisbon route, at first with this Boeing 707-321 (pictured previously in Turkish Airlines guise) and later with a Boeing 720-023. Both aircraft carried the registration C9-ARG, and both were leased from Tempair International Airlines. The 707-321 with registration C9-ARF was stored at Brussels Airport from September 1976, and was broken up in August 1980.

N716HH, a Boeing 707-321 of Italian airline Aeropa, at Rotterdam Airport, Zestienhoven, on 8 May 1974, together with her sister aircraft I-SAVE, a Boeing 707-131. First flown in August 1959, and delivered to Pan American World Airways as N716PA *Clipper Flying Eagle*, this aircraft was then leased to Turkish Airlines from May 1972 to May 1973 as TC-JAN, before being sub-leased to JAT (Yugoslav Airlines) as YU-AGH for several months. Aeropa was the next leaseholder, in April 1974, before the aircraft was repossessed by Pan Am in March 1975. It was then leased to Aerovias Quisqueyana (Dominican Republic), and was bought by British Midland Airways in May 1977 for spares, before being broken up at Stansted Airport in September 1977.

9G-ACD, Biman Bangladesh Airlines Boeing 707-321, seen stored at Ostend Airport on 30 January 1977. Biman Bangladesh is the national airline of the state of Bangladesh, established on 4 January 1972. Scheduled passenger service started with a twice-weekly service to London Heathrow with a Boeing 707-331, S2-ABM, which was leased from Air Manila International from September to December 1973. In December 1973, Biman Bangladesh bought S2-ABM, before leasing several other Boeing 707s from Tempair International Airlines, including 9G-ACD. Originally delivered to Pan American as N725PA in December 1959, this aircraft was also leased to several other airlines, such as Turkish Airlines, Geminair, DETA and Somali Airlines. It was placed in storage at Miami in 1984 before being broken up.

RP-C7074, Boeing 707-321 of Air Manila International, pictured at Manila International Airport in May 1976. Delivered to Pan American World Airways in January 1960 as N726PA *Clipper Westward Ho*, this aircraft was leased to Dominicana and Aeronauts International, and was repossessed by Pan Am in April 1975. It was sold to Air Manila International in June 1975 as RP-C7074 *Gregorio de Pilar*. Air Manila was formed in 1964, operating domestic services using two DC-3s. In 1974, Air Manila began scheduled and charter flights to the United States with five Boeing 707s. Air Manila later merged with Philippine Airlines.

N731JP, Aerovias Quisqueyana (Dominican Republic) Boeing 707-321, at Miami International Airport in March 1976. The Dominican airline operated Lockheed Constellations on passenger and cargo services linking Santo Domingo to San Juan, Puerto Rico, in the late 1970s. Aerovias Quisqueyana leased a Boeing 707 for a service from Santo Domingo to Miami, Florida, from March 1974. Originally built for Pan American World Airways as N729PA *Clipper Isabella*, the aircraft was leased to Turkish Airlines as TC-JAM, and then Trans Panama as N427MA. It was subsequently stored at Miami International Airport in November 1980, before being broken up in July 1983.

OO-SJA, Sabena Boeing 707-329 front fuselage section, at the Brussels Air Museum in December 2009. This aircraft was the first Boeing 707 ordered by a European operator, the order being placed by Sabena on 28 December 1958. The aircraft was delivered on 4 December 1959 as OO-SJA. During its lifetime, the aircraft was leased to Tunis Air, Air Algerie, Mandala Airlines, Sobelair and Cameroon Airlines, before returning to Sabena. On 1 June 1981, OO-SJA's Certificate of Airworthiness expired, its registration was cancelled, and it was donated to the Brussels Air Museum in April 1982. Only the front fuselage section was assembled, due to lack of space in the museum. The aircraft's total recorded flying hours amounted to 64,463hrs 25min.

OO-SJA, Sabena Boeing 707-329, flying from Brussels Airport to Tel Aviv as SN203 with co-pilot Jean Marie Colson on 25 December 1979. On 16 July 1960, this aircraft carried 303 passengers from Leopoldville, Congo, to Brussels as part of the Congo Airlift following unrest after the country became independent from Belgium. The record-setting non-stop flight of 4,000 miles took seven hours, and was within safe limits because many of the passengers were children and babies, with a breakdown of 12 men, 131 women, 118 children, 32 babies, plus a crew of ten. Most children sat on the floor, and babies were placed safely in luggage racks. During the Congo Airlift, Sabena aircraft made a total of 62 flights, with an average of 250 passengers on each flight. (Michel Anciaux)

G-BFMI, Boeing 707-123 of Monarch Airlines, seen at Luton Airport on 7 August 1978. Monarch Airlines undertook inclusive-tour flights and worldwide charter services from its home base at Luton Airport. The company was formed on 5 June 1967, initially flying two Bristol Britannias. Monarch's first two Boeing 720s arrived in November 1971 and April 1972. G-BFMI was delivered to American Airlines as N7505A in January 1959, and bought by Monarch Airlines in February 1978. It was then sold to Cyprus Airways as 5B-DAK in February 1979, and was seen in storage at Larnaca Airport, Cyprus, in 1983, before being broken up.

5B-DAP, Cyprus Airways Boeing 707-123, at Dusseldorf Airport on 3 October 1980. Cyprus Airways began operations on 4 April 1971 using Hawker Siddeley Tridents, later followed by two Boeing 720-023Bs leased from Monarch Airlines in 1978. Delivered to American Airlines as N7508A in March 1959, 5B-DAP was sold to Cyprus Airways, which operated the aircraft from February 1980 to May 1989. It was then bought by Omega Air as EL-AJV in June 1989, before being sold back to Boeing for the KC-135 tanker programme in August 1990. It was broken up 2002.

HK-1818, Boeing 707-123 of Aerocondor Colombia, seen at Miami International Airport on 31 October 1978. This aircraft was delivered to American Airlines in April 1959, as N7510A *Flagship Massachusetts*, and was sold to Paninternational as D-ALAM in November 1970, before being bought by Aerocondor in March 1976. It was placed in storage in 1979, and broken up at El Dorado Airport, Bogotá, in 1988. Aerocondor was formed in February 1955 for Colombian domestic flights, initially using Lockheed L-188A/F Electras. The company later bought two Boeing 720s and two Boeing 707s for international cargo and passenger services.

N702PC, Ports of Call Boeing 707-123, pictured at Stansted Airport on 15 August 1984. Delivered to American Airlines as N7518A in July 1959, this 707 was bought by Ports of Call in August 1980, remaining in service until May 1987. It was then sold to Boeing, stored at Davis-Monthan AFB, Arizona, and used for parts in the KC-135 programme. It had been broken up by the late 1980s. Ports of Call was a travel club with over 66,000 members, based at Denver, Colorado, which traded from 1967 until 1992, operating flights all over the world.

PH-TVA, Boeing 707-123 of Transavia Holland, at Schiphol Airport, Amsterdam, on 23 May 1981. This aircraft was delivered to American Airlines as N7519A *Flagship Kentucky* in August 1959, and was bought by Transavia Holland in March 1972. Transavia used the Boeing 707 mainly for charters to Southern Europe, but also to the United States and Canada. This particular aircraft was leased to a number of airlines, such as Royal Air Maroc, Saudi Arabian Airlines and Trans Oceanic Airways. It was bought by Guy America Airways in May 1982, and sold the following year to Boeing. It was then stored at Davis-Monthan AFB, and its parts were used in the KC-135 programme.

C-GQBG, Boeing 707-123B of Quebecair, seen at Paris Orly Airport on 18 June 1979. Originally delivered on 12 August 1959 to American Airlines, with registration N7520A, this aircraft was sold to Quebecair in November 1974 as C-GQBG, remaining in service with the Canadian airline until December 1978. It was then bought by World Jet Aviation and stored at Luxemburg Airport, before being sold to United African Airlines as 5A-DHO in September 1980, and re-registered as 5A-DHM. It was broken up at Brussels Airport in August 1984.

N735T, Boeing 707-131 of Club International, at Schiphol Airport, Amsterdam, on 19 June 1971. This 707 was delivered to Trans World Airlines on 18 April 1959 as N735TW. It was bought by Club International on 9 March 1971, and was operated as N735T before being sold to Aero America on 31 March 1975. It was withdrawn from use in June 1981 and broken up. Club International became the first travel club to operate jet aircraft, and was based at Boeing Field, Seattle. The company's first trans-Atlantic flight was to Schiphol on 18 June 1971.

HB-IEG, Boeing 707-131 of Phoenix Airways (Switzerland), seen at Schiphol Airport, Amsterdam, on 28 April 1974. This short-lived airline operated from 1970 to 1974, using two Boeing 707s and two BAC 1-11s. Operating primarily from Basel Airport, the company ran charters to southern Europe, Thailand and Togo. This aircraft was ordered by Trans World Airlines in July 1959 as N744TW, then served with Phoenix Airways from November 1972 to 1974. It was leased to several airlines, including Fragtflug, ARCA Colombia, Air India and Lloyd Aéro Boliviano. It crashed during take-off from Viru Viru Airport, Santa Cruz, Bolivia, on 13 October 1976.

N702PT, Boeing 707-331 operated by Perfect Air Tours, seen at Stansted Airport on 7 August 1978. Perfect Air Tours was owned by three Egyptian brothers (though a US corporation), and was formed to run inclusive tours throughout Africa from Cairo. Delivered to Pan American World Airways as N702PA *Clipper Hotspur* in December 1959, this aircraft was then bought by Transatlantic Airways in December 1974, and sold to Perfect Air Tours in April 1975. It was stored at Stansted from January 1976, and was broken up in 1980.

N703PA, Boeing 707-331 operated by Filipinas Orient Airways, at Miami International Airport on 5 November 1971. Filipinas Orient was founded in 1964 and operated domestic flights in the Philippines with a DC3, Caravelle, Nord 262 and a NAMC YS-11. The company bought this ex-Pan American 707-331 in September 1971 for flights to Thailand, Vietnam and the US, but the sale was subsequently cancelled. Eventually, the Boeing 707 was sold to Air Manila International in December 1973 as PI-C7073, and was placed in storage at Manila International Airport in February 1982.

D-ADAP, Boeing 707-138 of Air Commerz, seen at Dusseldorf Airport on 22 October 1971. Air Commerz was founded in 1970 and operated until 1972, with bases at Dusseldorf and Hamburg Airports. The company's fleet consisted of two Boeing 707s, and two Vickers Viscounts. The 707 pictured was originally delivered to Qantas Airways in June 1959.

N790SA, Boeing 707-138 of Standard Airways, at London Gatwick Airport on 30 July 1967. Delivered to Qantas Airways as VH-EBB *City of Sydney* on 26 June 1959, this aircraft was later converted to Boeing 707-138B specification; the 'B' model suffix indicating that the aircraft was powered by Pratt and Whitney JT3D turbofans. Qantas sold the 707 to Seymour R Gross, who leased the Boeing to Standard Airways, Seattle, as N790SA from June 1967 to August 1968. The aircraft later passed through various other airlines and leasing companies, including Turkish Airlines, Pan Ayer, Jet Aviation, Lowa, Jetran and Comtran International, and was re-registered as N138SR in November 1990. It was leased by the Congo Government for a period from April 1994, and then transferred to Jaffe Group Inc. The aircraft was damaged beyond repair in a hangar fire, following an arson attack at Port Harcourt Airport, Nigeria, on 5 September 1998.

G-AVZZ, International Caribbean Airways Boeing 707-138B, at Luxembourg Airport on 30 July 1973. International Caribbean Airways was formed in September 1970, and began a weekly scheduled service between Barbados Grantley Adams International Airport and Luxembourg Airport in December 1970, later routed via London Gatwick Airport. The airline's fleet was wet-leased from Laker Airways, the principal shareholder. Qantas Airways originally took delivery of this aircraft as VH-EBD in August 1959, and it was converted to 138B specification in November 1961, before being sold to British Eagle International Airlines as G-AVZZ in January 1968. It was sold to Laker Airways in February 1969, and leased to International Caribbean Airways in December 1970. It was later sold to Charlotte Aircraft Corporation. The aircraft was stored at Paris Le Bourget Airport from December 1978, and was broken up in July 1983.

VH-EBG, Boeing 707-138 of Qantas Airways, at Schiphol Airport, Amsterdam, in April 1966. This aircraft was delivered to Qantas as VH-EBG *City of Hobart* on 18 September 1959, and was sold to British Eagle International Airlines in March 1968, operated as G-AWDG. It was quickly sold to Laker Airways in January 1969, then bought by Charlotte Aircraft Corporation and re-registered as N600JJ in November 1978. It later passed through several operators, including IASCO, Sheikh Abdallah Baroom, and Skyways Aircraft Inc. It was sold to the government of the Democratic Republic of Congo as 9Q-CLK in March 1998, and was later used by President Kabila as his private aircraft.

G-APFG, Boeing 707-436 of BEA Air Tours, at Hellinikon Airport, Athens, on 6 April 1973. BEA Airtours was formed on 24 April 1969 as a division of British European Airways, to provide the airline with a low-cost platform to participate in the fast-growing inclusive-tour holiday flights market, which until then had been the exclusive domain of independent privately owned airlines, rather than government-subsidised national carriers. This aircraft was delivered to BOAC as G-APFG on 23 June 1960, and was leased to BEA Airtours in March 1973. BEA Air Tours was rebranded as British Airtours in April 1974. The aircraft was sold to Aviation Traders Ltd in March 1981, and in later years, the UK Civil Aviation Authority used it for fire suppression tests at Stansted Airport, before it was broken up in 1991.

G-APFJ, Malaysia Air Lines Boeing 707-436, at London Heathrow Airport in September 1972. Delivered to BOAC in September 1960, this aircraft was leased to Malaysia-Singapore Airlines (MSA) from 4 November 1971, before the carrier changed its name to Malaysia Air Lines in September 1972. G-APFJ was returned to British Airways (formerly BOAC) in April 1975, then leased to British Airtours. It was bought by the Cosford Aerospace Museum in June 1981.

G-APFL, Boeing 707-436 of Syrian Arab Airlines, at Munich-Riem Airport in June 1974. G-AFPL was delivered to BOAC on 21 October 1960, then leased to BOAC Cunard, BEA Airtours and British Airtours. Syrian Arab Airlines leased the 707 from April 1974 to July 1975, before it was sold to Cargo Charter Airways as 9Q-CRW in March 1980. In January 1981, it was sold to Coastal Airways as 5X-CAU, and then passed through Aero Equipment during 1982, before it was withdrawn from use and stored at Entebbe Airport, Uganda. Today the aircraft rests in a dilapidated state just outside Entebbe Airport perimeter fence, near the aptly named Aero Beach restaurant.

9G-ACK, Boeing 707-430 operated by Geminair, seen at Manston Airport on 26 April 1979. Geminair (Gemini Air Transport), formed in 1974, and based in Ghana, operated cargo charter flights throughout the African continent and beyond. It flew a regular service between the Ghanaian capital, Accra, and Luton, inaugurated on 7 May 1976 with an ex-Royal Air Force Bristol Britannia. The 707 was originally delivered to Lufthansa in October 1960 as D-ABOF, and was bought by Geminair in August 1977. It was then leased to several other airlines, such as DETA Mozambique, Sabena and Egyptair, before being sold in July 1981 to Bata International Airways (Equatorial Guinea) as 3C-ABI. In 1983, it was sold to Liberian Overseas Airways as EL-AJC, but was withdrawn from use and stored at Bournemouth Hurn Airport, before being broken up in August 1983.

6O-SAW, Boeing 720-023B of Somali Airlines, at Schiphol Airport, Amsterdam, on 5 September 1978. During the 1970s, Somali Airlines operated scheduled passenger and cargo services from the Somali capital, Mogadishu, to Rome, Jeddah, Nairobi and Cairo, with two Boeing 720-023Bs. This aircraft was delivered to American Airlines as *Flagship Wisconsin* with registration N7529A in August 1960, and was converted to 720-023B specification in September 1961. It was withdrawn from use in July 1971, and stored for several years at Tulsa International Airport, Oklahoma. It was bought by Somali Airlines, on 7 May 1976, and operated until August 1983, when it was broken up at Mogadishu Airport, Somalia.

OD-AFW, Boeing 720-023B of Middle East Airlines (MEA), photographed at Hellinikon Airport, Athens, on 8 April 1973. Middle East Airlines was formed in Lebanon in 1945, and in 1963 the company merged with Air Liban. In 1977, MEA's Boeing fleet consisted of three Boeing 707-384s and 14 Boeing 720-023Bs, plus three Boeing 747-2B4Bs. This aircraft was delivered to American Airlines in February 1961 as N7540A *Flagship Kansas*, and was sold to Middle East Airlines as OD-AFW in March 1972. It was then leased to Nigeria Airways and Libyan Arab Airlines, before returning to Beirut in May 1977. An Israeli attack on Beirut International Airport on 12 June 1977 resulted in six MEA Boeing 707 and 720 aircraft being destroyed, including OD-AFW.

HC-BDP, Boeing 720-023B of Ecuatoriana (Ecuador), at Mariscal Sucre International Airport, Quito, on 28 October 1977. Ecuatoriana dazzled the aviation world with a series of special liveries during the 1970s, including this example, seen at the 2,800m (9,186ft)-above-sea-level Mariscal Sucre Airport. HC-BDP was originally ordered by American Airlines in May 1961 as N7547A, and was leased to Pan Am as N780PA in 1963, and then to Ecuatoriana as HC-AZO. It was later converted to Boeing 720-023B(F) specification and registered as HC-BDP in April 1977. It was withdrawn from use at Miami International Airport in December 1984, and bought by Boeing for the KC-135 programme, moving to Davis-Monthan AFB, where it was dismantled.

HC-AZP, Boeing 720-023B operated by Ecuatoriana (Ecuador), pictured at Jorge Chavez Airport, Lima, on 2 November 1977. Another amazing livery is visible on this Ecuatoriana Boeing 720-023B, arriving at Lima Airport. At the time, all Boeings in service with Ecuatoriana had unique colour schemes. This 720 was delivered to American Airlines in July 1961, and leased to Pan American as N781PA in March 1963. Pan Am then bought the aircraft in April 1964 and operated it as *Clipper Flying Arrow*. It was bought by Ecuatoriana in March 1975, and registered HC-AZP. Later, it was stored at Marana Pinal Air Park, Arizona, and broken up in May 1988.

HC-AZQ, Boeing 720-023B of Ecuatoriana (Ecuador), at Guayaquil International Airport, Ecuador, on 28 October 1977. Ecuatoriana was the national carrier of Ecuador, which was set up in July 1974, beginning with international services to North, Central and South America, and later Spain. The airline ceased operations in 2006. Some of the Ecuatoriana 707s and 720s became flying canvases for abstract artwork, and these distinctively painted aircraft were seen as a response to a number of aircraft operated by Braniff in bright abstract liveries designed by artist Alexander Calder. Ordered by American Airlines in July 1961 as N7551A, this aircraft was bought by Pan American in May 1964, and operated as N782PA. It was sold to Doral Trading in September 1974, and leased to Ecuatoriana as HC-AZQ in January 1975. Finally, it was bought by Boeing in October 1984 and placed into storage at Davis-Monthan AFB, to be dismantled for use in the KC-135 programme.

HP-685, Boeing 720-022 of Inair Panama, seen at Tocumen Airport, Panama, on 10 December 1973. Inair Panama (Internacional de Aviacion) was a wholly-Panamanian-owned organisation and was founded as a charter company in January 1967. The company flew regular cargo flights to various destinations in Central and South America, originally with four Douglas DC6s and a Lockheed L-188AF Electra. Two Boeing 720-022s were bought in the autumn of 1973, for a cargo service to Miami. Originally ordered by United Air Lines in December 1960, as N7212U, this aircraft was bought by Inair in September 1973 as HP-685. It was leased to West African Ventures, and returned in October 1975, before being re-registered as N37777 and leased to H. Schiro and Gulf Miles Co. On 22 April 1976, while on lease to US Global, the aircraft was carrying 19 tonnes of flowers on an internal Colombian flight from El Dorado Airport, Bogotá, to Barranquilla, when it crashed near Barranquilla due to poor runway lighting.

HK-676, Boeing 720-030B operated by SAM Colombia, at El Dorado Airport, Bogotá, in November 1977. SAM was established on 6 October 1945 as an all-cargo operator. In 1962, the company bought several Lockheed L-188A Electras for domestic passenger services in Colombia, and three Boeing 720-030Bs were purchased in 1977, when SAM became a subsidiary of Avianca (Colombia). Delivered to Lufthansa in May 1961 as D-ABOL, this aircraft was sold to Pan American as N784PA in March 1964, and was then sold to Avianca in April 1973 as HK-676. It was leased to SAM Colombia in March 1977, and was bought by Boeing in August 1983 and broken up for the KC-135 programme.

N7225U, Boeing 720-022, in Sierra Trans Air livery, at Boeing Field, Seattle, on 4 July 1986. Originally delivered to United Airlines as N7225U *Mainliner Walter T Varney* in April 1962, this aircraft was leased to the Jet Set Travel Club in October 1973, and the company then bought the 720 in November 1978. It was sold to Sierra Trans Air in September 1986, and leased to Pan African Express (Zaire) in November 1986. It was then sold to ACS (Air Charter Service), based in Zaire, as 9Q-CTM. ACS had two Hawker Siddeley Trident 3Bs in service, and the Boeing 720-022 was used for spares for other Boeings in Zaire. It was broken up in the 1990s at Ndjili Airport, Kinshasa, Zaire (now the Democratic Republic of Congo).

N707HD, Boeing 707-321 of Age of Enlightenment Aviation, seen at Beek Airport, Maastricht, on 17 April 1985. Delivered to Pan American on 23 August 1961 as N758PA, this 707 was leased to Lloyd International as G-AYRZ, and Lloyd subsequently bought the aircraft in January 1971. It then passed through several operators, including Bahamas World, MCA Leasing, Southeast Airlines and Quantum Leasing, before it was bought by Age of Enlightenment Aviation in July 1984. It was sold to the Benin government as TY-AAM in July 1987, and re-registered as TY-BBW in November 1987. After being stored at Ostend Airport from May 1989, it was later sold to a private owner and parked at Wetteren, Belgium, along the N400 road between Ostend and Brussels.

VP-BDF, Boeing 707-321 of Bahamas World Airways, at London Stansted Airport on 24 February 1973. Bahamas World Airways was founded in 1968, but did not start operations until November 1971, initially with a Boeing 707-138, and then in December 1972 two additional Boeing 707-321s, based at Nassau. Ordered by Pan American in June 1961 as N759PA *Clipper Texas*, this aircraft was then leased by Lloyd International Airways in March 1970 as G-AYAG, and was bought by Bahamas World Airways in December 1972 as VP-BDF. It was repossessed by the Commonwealth Bank (Bahamas) in September 1974, and was eventually broken up at Dublin Airport in July 1984.

HK-724, Avianca (Colombia) Boeing 720-059B, at Miami International Airport on 20 November 1980. Avianca (Aerovias del Continente Americanao SA) was founded on 5 December 1919, and its international network provides extensive passenger and cargo services throughout North, Central and South America, and to the Caribbean and Europe. HK-724 was one of three Boeing 720-059Bs ordered by the company, and was delivered on 8 November 1961. It was operated by Avianca for 22 years, and was sold in July 1983 to Monarch Aviation as N4451B. It was placed in storage at Miami International Airport in November 1983, and had been broken up by November 1985.

OO-TEA, Boeing 720-025 of TEA (Trans European Airways), seen at Brussels Airport, Zaventem, on 6 August 1977. Trans European Airways operated an all-jet fleet on worldwide charter and inclusive-tour flights from Brussels Airport. The airline was formed in October 1970 by the Belgian tour operator TIFA and Georges P Gutelman, and flights commenced in 1971 with an ex-Eastern Air Lines Boeing 720-025. Delivered to Prudential in August 1961 as N8702E, this 720 was leased to EAL (Eastern Air Lines), which bought the aircraft in October 1966. It was then sold to TEA in April 1971, before being stored at Brussels Airport in November 1977, and broken up in October 1980.

LN-TUW, Boeing 720-025 of Trans Polar Air Service, seen at Gando Airport, Las Palmas (Gran Canaria), on 6 December 1970. Trans Polar Air Services was a Norwegian charter airline that operated between June 1970 and May 1971, using three Boeing B720s, with registrations LN-TUU, TUV and TUW. Delivered to Prudential as N8704E in September 1961, this aircraft was then operated by EAL (Eastern Air Lines), before being sold to Trans Polar in May 1970. It returned to Boeing in 1971, was registered as N8704E, and was modified as an ASW (Anti-Submarine Warfare) test aircraft in August 1975, with registration N40102. It was later stored at Kingman Airport, Arizona, and broken up in 1977.

HL-7403, Boeing 720-025 operated by Korean Air Lines, seen at Kingman Airport, Arizona, on 15 November 1978. Korean Air Lines was formed in June 1962 by the government of South Korea as a successor to Korean National Airlines. Beginning in 1969, Korean Air Lines operated flights to Hong Kong, Japan, Taiwan and Los Angeles, initially with Boeing 707s and 720s, until the introduction of the Boeing 747 in 1973. HL-7403 was originally ordered by Prudential in October 1961, and leased as N8710E to Eastern Air Lines, which bought the aircraft in October 1966. It was then sold to Korean Air Lines in January 1970, operating as HL-7403 until October 1977. It was flown to Kingman Airport, Arizona, for storage in November 1977, and was broken up in 1980.

61-0282, Boeing EC-135H Stratotanker of the USAF, seen at RAF Mildenhall on 31 July 1977. While the 707 and 720 were revolutionising the civil transport scene, Boeing was delivering hundreds of KC-135s to the USAF. The first of these tankers entered service on 18 June 1957, and deliveries of tankers and other military variants continued until January 1965, by which time 820 aircraft had been handed over. 61-0282, a KC-135A, first flew on 9 January 1962. In June 1962, the aircraft was converted to an EC-135A NEACP (National Emergency Airborne Command Post), and was based at RAF Mildenhall, UK, with the 10th ACCS (Airborne Command and Control Squadron). In 1989, it was re-engined and modified to EC-135H specification, before later being allocated to the USAF Medical Readiness Training Center, San Antonio, Texas, as a GEC-135H ground instructional trainer.

OE-IEB, Boeing 707-321B of Flyglob Handels GmbH, seen at Paris Le Bourget Airport on 13 June 1981. Delivered to Pan American in June 1962 as N764PA *Clipper Nautilus*, this aircraft was taken out of service in December 1976 and stored at Miami Airport, before being bought by ATASCO Leasing in August 1977 as N764SE. It was leased to Flyglob Handels GmbH from January 1979, and was bought in June 1989 by Omega Air as N897WA. It was sold to Boeing in September 1989 for the KC-135 tanker programme.

SX-DBH, Boeing 720-051B of Olympic Airways, at Hellinikon Airport, Athens, on 6 April 1973. Olympic Airways was established on 1 January 1957, when the Greek ship-owner Aristotle Onassis acquired the assets of the national Greek airline, TAE. Olympic Airways inaugurated services on 6 April 1957 with domestic routes, followed on 2 May with services from Athens to Rome, Paris and London, operating a Douglas DC-6B. The first Boeing 720s arrived in March and April 1972. This aircraft was delivered to Northwest Orient Airlines as N723US on 11 July 1961, bought by Olympic Airways in March 1972 and was in service until December 1979. It was broken up in Athens in 1985.

OE-LBA, Boeing 707-329 operated by Austrian Airlines, seen at Brussels Airport, Zaventem, on 3 August 1969. This aircraft was originally ordered by Sabena in April 1962, then leased to Air Congo, and subsequently Austrian Airlines as OE-LBA in April 1969. It returned to Sabena in September 1971 as OO-SJF. It was then leased to Air Algérie and Mandala Airlines, before being bought by Israel Aircraft Industries (IAI) as 4X-BYL on 19 January 1977. It was operated by the Israeli Air Force from June 1977 as 4X-JYL, code 128, and was then stored at Tel Aviv Airport and broken up.

AP-AMG, Boeing 720-040B of Air Malta, at Paris Orly Airport on 22 March 1977. Delivered to PIA (Pakistan International Airlines) as AP-AMG in December 1961, this 720 was leased to Air Malta from 29 March 1974 to 21 March 1979. It was withdrawn from use at Malta Airport in October 1981, and was later used by the Malta Fire Department for training at the airport, before being broken up in 1997.

G-ARRC, Boeing 707-436 of British Airtours, pictured at London Gatwick Airport on 1 August 1980. This aircraft was delivered to BOAC-Cunard in March 1963 as G-ARRC, before BOAC merged with BEA (British European Airways) to form British Airways in April 1974. The aircraft was then leased to Air Mauritius and British Airtours, before entering storage at London Stansted Airport in November 1980. It was bought by Europe Aéro Service (EAS), and flown to Perpignan, France, in March 1981. It then passed through several owners, including Cobra Airways in 1983 and ACS (Air Charter Service), as 9Q-CTK, in 1989. It was broken up at Kinshasa Airport, Zaire (now the Democratic Republic of Congo), in April 1995.

OY-APW, Boeing 720-051B operated by Maersk Air, pictured at Salzburg Airport, Austria, in January 1980. Originally delivered to Northwest Orient Airlines in December 1961 as N729US, this Boeing 720 was leased from Boeing before being purchased, serving with Northwest Orient from May 1962 to January 1973. It was then sold to Maersk Air as OY-APW in March 1973, leased to Nigeria Airways and Tunis Air, and returned to Maersk Air in December 1979. It was bought by Conair of Scandinavia in February 1981, and remained in service until March 1987. It was sold to AirXport in March 1987 as TF-AYB. One month later, it was bought by Boeing for spare parts for the KC-135 tanker programme, and was broken up by December 1990.

HZ-KA1, Boeing 720-047B, owned by Sheikh Kamal Adham, at Paris Le Bourget Airport on 26 June 1982. Delivered to Western Airlines in July 1962 as N93145, this aircraft remained in service with the airline until May 1978. It was bought by Saudi Sheikh Kamal Adham, as HZ-NAA, in August 1978 and re-registered as HZ-KA1 in June 1980. It was sold to Comtran International in December 1989 as N2143J, and was then bought by JAR Aircraft Services Inc in November 1991, and re-registered as N720JR. It was operated for the Republic of Congo government from 1998 to 1999, and for the Lebanese government during 2002, before being stored at Malta and scrapped in January 2018.

ET-AAH, Boeing 720-060B of Ethiopian Airlines, at Hellinikon Airport, Athens, on 6 April 1973. Ethiopian Airlines was founded on 26 December 1945 to develop an international service, and a collaboration agreement was signed with TWA. Operations began in 1946 with five surplus C-47s for domestic services, and for international services the company bought two 720-060Bs in November 1962, followed by four more between 1965 and 1975. ET-AAH was delivered in November 1962, and remained in service until December 1987. It was then flown to Marana Pinal Air Park, Arizona, and later to Davis-Monthan AFB, to be used for the KC-135 programme. It was broken up in the late 1990s.

G-BFBZ, Boeing 707-351B operated by Caribbean Airways, at London Gatwick Airport on 8 August 1978. Delivered to Northwest Orient Airlines on 19 June 1963 as N352US, this aircraft remained in service with Northwest until November 1971. It was bought by Cathay Pacific in December 1971, as VR-HGI, and left the Cathay fleet in October 1977. The 707 was then sold to Laker Airways (formed in 1966 by Freddie Laker, a former director of British United Airways) as G-BFBZ during November 1977. Finally, G-BFBZ was operated by Caribbean Airways from Gatwick to Bridgetown Barbados, before being stored at Lasham and broken up in 1986.

753, Boeing KC-135R of the Republic of Singapore Air Force, seen at Changi Airport, Singapore, on 21 March 2012. Boeing delivered the first of four re-engined KC-135R Stratotankers to the Republic of Singapore Air Force on 10 September 1999. This KC-135R, originally built as a KC-135A for the USAF, was modified with updated, fuel-efficient CFM56 engines and the Boeing-developed MPRS (Multi-Point Refuelling System) – the first aircraft to receive both modifications. All four KC-135Rs were withdrawn from use at Changi AFB in March 2020, and were sold to Meta Aerospace in the USA.

38470, Boeing C-135FR operated by the French Air Force, pictured at Eindhoven Airport on 31 March 2017. The Boeing C-135FR was introduced to French Air Force (Armée de l'Air) service in 1964, and a total of 12 were assigned to the French Strategic Air Forces, used mainly to support the nuclear-capable Mirage IVA. A C-135FR crashed near Hao Island Airport, Polynesia, during a deployment in June 1972, and the remaining aircraft were re-engined with CFM56 turbofans in the late 1980s. Three former USAF KC-135Rs were added to the French fleet in 1997, based at Istres-le Tubé Air Base.

5R-MFK, Boeing 707-328B of Air Madagascar, at Paris Orly Airport on 27 May 1973. Originally delivered to Air France in January 1964 as F-BLCB, this 707 was leased to Air Afrique and Air Madagascar, then bought by Air Madagascar which operated the aircraft from July 1973 to February 1979 as 5R-MFK. It was then sold back to Air France as F-BLLB, and passed through several other owners, including ATASCO, Libyan Arab Airlines (operated as 5A-DLT) and ZAS Airline of Egypt (operated as SU-DAJ). It was bought by Boeing in May 1987, as N83658, and used for the KC-135 programme before being broken up.

G-SAIL, Boeing 707-323C of Tradewinds Airways, pictured at Schiphol Airport, Amsterdam, on 7 April 1979. Delivered on 13 December 1963, as N7556A, to American Airlines, this aircraft remained in service with the US carrier until 1978. It was then bought by Tradewinds Airways in September 1978 as G-SAIL. Tradewinds Airlines was formed in November 1968, and operated its first commercial flight on 2 April 1969 from London Gatwick Airport to Brisbane, Australia. The company ceased operations on 28 September 1990. G-SAIL was withdrawn from use in August 1981, and was stored at Lasham Airport prior to being bought by Boeing for the KC-135 programme

N375WA, Boeing 707-373C of World Airways, at Schiphol Airport, Amsterdam, on 29 September 1970. This aircraft began its life with World Airways, and served with the carrier from September 1963 to February 1971 as N375WA. It was sold to Britannia Airways, as G-AYSI, on 28 February 1971, before being leased to British Caledonian and Singapore Airlines, returning to Britannia in January 1980. It was then sold to International Air Leases, and leased to Tampa (Colombia) as HK-2401X in April 1980. On a flight from Medellin Airport, Colombia, to Miami, the 707 suffered damage to the number-four engine, and returned to Medellin. It was decided to ferry the aircraft to Miami, but on 14 December 1983, during take-off the number-three engine failed, and the 707 banked steeply and crashed.

HC-BLY, Boeing 707-373C of SAETA (Ecuador), at Miami International Airport on 20 November 1990. This aircraft was ordered by TWA (Trans World Airways) and served with the carrier from November 1963 until August 1979 as N789TW. It was bought by Aeronautics & Astronautics in February 1981, and briefly leased to Aerotal Colombia as HK-2606X. It was re-registered as HP-1027, and bought by Ecuadorian carrier SAETA in July 1985. It was withdrawn from use in May 1993, and broken up at Quito Airport, Ecuador, during 1995.

OO-ABA, Boeing 707-351C of Abelag Airways, at Brussels Airport, Zaventem, on 20 May 1979. Delivered to Northwest Orient Airlines in April 1964 as N356US, this 707 was bought by Pacific Western Airlines in March 1973 as C-FPWJ. It was then bought by Abelag Airways (Belgium) in May 1979 as OO-ABA. Subsequently, the aircraft passed through a number of leasing companies and airlines, including Nigeria Airways, Air Belgium, Ontario Worldair, United African Airlines, Air Jamahiriya, Libyan Arab Airlines, ZAS Airline of Egypt, African Express Airways, Omega Air, Executive Aviation Service and Rainbow Cargo. The aircraft was on a test flight from Ilorin, Nigeria, in March 1992, when it made a gear-up landing and was written off. (Michel Anciaux)

3X-GAZ, Boeing 707-351C operated by Air Guinée, seen at Schiphol Airport, Amsterdam, on 24 April 1980. This aircraft was built for Northwest Orient Airlines as N358US in June 1964, and was sold to Cathay Pacific Airways as VR-HHD in March 1974. After five years in service with Cathay, it was bought by Omni Aircraft Sales in September 1979, and registered as 3X-GAZ for Air Guinée. The Guinea-based carrier used the aircraft for cargo flights from Conakry to Europe. It was then sold to the Aviation Consultants leasing company in July 1986 as N18AZ. It was leased to Lan-Chile as CC-CCE, and Angola Air Charter as D2-TOR, and returned to the leasing company in June 1998. After being stored at Addis Ababa Airport from December 1999, the aircraft was broken up in 2012. (Peter de Groot)

OY-APU, Boeing 720-051B of Conair of Scandinavia, at Malaga Airport on 18 October 1984. Conair of Scandinavia A/S was a Danish charter airline, formed in October 1964. It was the successor to Flying Enterprise, and began operations in March 1965 with five Douglas DC-7s. The company acquired four Boeing 720s in 1971 to undertake charters mainly to points in the Mediterranean. Originally ordered by Northwest Orient Airlines as N736US in June 1964, this aircraft was sold to Maersk Air in April 1974 as OY-APU, and bought by Conair in April 1981. It was then acquired by Boeing, in May 1987, for the KC-135 programme.

N707GB, Boeing 707-338C of Arrow Air, at Miami International Airport on 26 October 1981. Delivered to Qantas as VH-EBN in February 1965, this 707 left the fleet in June 1974, and was sold to Singapore Airlines as 9V-BFW, serving with the airline until April 1981. It was then bought by International Air Leases, as N707GA, and leased to several airlines such as Arrow Air, Tampa (Colombia – as HK-3030X), and Skymaster Airlines (as PT-WSZ). It was later stored at Viracopas Airport, São Paulo, before being preserved on a ranch near Campinas, Brazil.

5N-ARQ, Boeing 707-338C operated by GAS Air Cargo, seen at Schiphol Airport, Amsterdam, on 6 April 1984. This 707 was originally delivered to Qantas Airways in March 1965 as VH-EBO, then sold to Singapore Airlines, which operated the aircraft from November 1972 to February 1981 as 9V-BFN. It was then bought by International Air Leases, as N4225J, and subsequently passed through several leasing companies and airlines, including Arrow Air, RN Cargo of Nigeria, Dairo Air Services and LAC (Lignes Aériennes Congolaises). Allied Airlines bought the 707 in August 1999 as 5N-ARQ. It was later withdrawn from use and stored at Manston Airport, before being broken up in 2001.

SU-BBA, Boeing 707-338C of Air Cargo Egypt, at Schiphol Airport, Amsterdam, on 2 April 1979. Delivered to Qantas Airways as VH-EBP *City of Alice Springs* in August 1965, this aircraft was the 16th new Boeing 707 delivered to Qantas. It was sold to TWA, and served with the carrier as N14791 from November 1972 to February 1979, and was then bought by Air Cargo Egypt in March 1979 as SU-BBA. It operated its final revenue-earning service, from London Gatwick to Cairo, on 17 March 1982, by which time the aircraft had flown 42,610 hours. It was withdrawn from use at Cairo Airport, and was observed being used as a restaurant near the airport in December 1994, but was scrapped in December 2003.

AP-AXL, Boeing 720-047B in PIA (Pakistan International Airlines) livery, at Schiphol Airport, Amsterdam, on 14 September 1981. PIA was formed in 1951 as the state carrier, and began services with a Super Constellation on 7 June 1954, providing a valuable connection between east and west Pakistan. International routes to Cairo and London followed in February 1955. The first Boeing 720s arrived in 1961 and 1962. Ordered by Western Airlines and delivered in September 1964 as N93152, this aircraft left the Western Airlines fleet after ten years, and was bought by PIA as AP-AXL in August 1974. It was withdrawn from use in August 1986, and was displayed at the PIA Planetarium in Lahore.

Above: ZP-CCE, Boeing 707-321B of LAP (Lineas Aereas Paraguayas), at Asunción Airport on 19 November 1988. Originally delivered to Pan American as N410PA *Clipper Argonaut* in April 1965, this aircraft remained in service with Pan Am until September 1978. It was sold to ATASCO Leasing in October 1978, and was leased to LAP on 20 October 1978, arriving at Asunción Airport, Paraguay, on 10 November 1978. Two more Boeing 707s followed, in 1978 and 1980. LAP was formed in 1962 as the national airline of Paraguay, and began services with two Convair 240s, later followed by three Lockheed L-188 Electras.

Right: The author was very lucky to be able to fly in an LAP (Lineas Aereas Paraguayas) Boeing 707-321B, ZP-CCE, from Santiago, Chile, to Asunción, Paraguay. The flight crossed the Andes mountains, home of the highest peak in the Western Hemisphere – the 6,961m (22,838ft) Mount Aconcagua. Here is a beautiful view of the mountains, but also of the Boeing 707-321B's engines. The intercontinental version of the 707 – the 320 series – was somewhat larger than its predecessors. Powered by four JT4A engines, it had an increased fuel capacity, which gave it a still-air range of 5,860 miles (9,431km) with a payload of 21,400lb (9,707kg).

TC-JBU, Boeing 707-321B of Turkish Airlines, pictured at Schiphol Airport, Amsterdam, on 6 September 1981. Delivered to Pan American in May 1965, as N412PA *Clipper Empress of the Skies*, this aircraft left Pan Am service in May 1978, and was sold to ATASCO Leasing. It was leased to Turkish Airlines on 19 June 1978 as TC-JBU, returning to ATASCO in February 1985 as N5517Z. It was then bought by Boeing in January 1986, for use in the KC-135 programme. Turkish Airlines was a major Boeing 707 operator, with many examples in service between 1971 and 1978.

EI-ANO, Boeing 707-348C of Aer Lingus, at Newcastle Airport in June 1967. Aer Lingus was formed in May 1936, and started operations from Dublin across the Irish Sea to Bristol (Whitchurch), using a de Havilland DH84 Dagon. In 1947, Aerlinte Eireann was set up to provide international services across the Atlantic to New York, and the operations of the two companies were fully integrated under the Aer Lingus name in 1960. Aer Lingus operated Boeing 707 variants from 1968 to 1986. Three Boeing 720-048s were delivered in 1961 covering the routes from Dublin and Shannon to New York and Boston.

5A-DIX, Boeing 707-348C of United African Airlines, pictured at Schiphol Airport, Amsterdam, on 31 January 1984. Originally delivered to Aer Lingus as EI-ANO in April 1965, this aircraft was leased to Flying Tiger Line as N318F from September 1966 to April 1968, and to Nigeria Airways in 1972. It returned to Aer Lingus in March 1973, and was then bought by United African Airlines in May 1981 as 5A-DIX. United African became Jamahiriya Air Transport in June 1983, and then Libyan Arab Airlines in June 1986. The 707 was sold to National Overseas Airlines in September 1992 as SU-BLJ, and was later withdrawn from use at Cairo and broken up in 2009.

OO-SJH, Boeing 707-329C of Sabena, at Brussels Airport, Zaventem, on 19 June 1979. Delivered to Sabena on 17 April 1965 as OO-SJH, this aircraft was leased to Air India in March 1976 for three months, and returned to Sabena in June 1976. It was then leased to TAG International and Air Zaire, before returning to Sabena in October 1979. Another lease followed, in March 1980, to Zaire International Cargo. During a flight from Paris Orly to Douala, Cameroon, on 11 May 1980, the 707 encountered windshear on short finals, resulting in a hard landing, followed by undercarriage collapse. The left wing broke in two, and two engines separated, resulting in the aircraft being damaged beyond repair.

N8725T, Boeing 707-331B of TWA (Trans World Airways), at Paris Charles de Gaulle Airport on 18 June 1979. Delivered to TWA on 12 January 1966 as N8725T, this aircraft served with the airline for 16 years, before entering storage at Kansas City Airport in December 1982. Boeing bought the 707 for the KC-135 programme, and it was flown to Davis-Monthan AFB and was broken up in 2013. TWA's origins date back to Western Air Express, which started operations in 1925. Transcontinental and Western Airlines was formed in October 1930, and TWA was rebranded as Trans World Airlines in the 1950s.

5N-ASY, Boeing 707-351C in the livery of EAS (Executive Airlines Services) Cargo Airlines, pictured at Ostend Airport on 19 August 1988. Originally delivered to Northwest Orient Airlines on 15 September 1965 as N362US, this aircraft left the fleet in October 1972, and was bought by Cathay Pacific Airways as VR-HGP in November 1972. The 707 then passed through many operators and leasing companies, including Nigeria Airways, United Air Services, EAS Cargo Airlines, Omega Air, Foremost Aviation, Impala Air, Trans Brasil, Amed Air and Brasair Transportes Aéreos. It returned to Omega Air in June 1996, and was withdrawn from use at Shannon Airport, Ireland, and broken up in 2003.

Z-WKS, Boeing 707-330B of Air Zimbabwe, at Harare Airport on 8 December 1993. This aircraft was originally delivered to Lufthansa, as D-ABUB *Stuttgart*, on 4 August 1965, and was then bought by Air Zimbabwe on 8 May 1981 as VP-WKS. It was re-registered as Z-WKS in October 1983, and withdrawn from use at Harare Airport in November 1997. Air Zimbabwe, formerly Air Rhodesia, came into being in 1979 following the renaming of its home country. Air Rhodesia was originally formed as a subsidiary of Central African Airways in June 1964, and became an independent corporation on 1 September 1967. The airline bought three Boeing 720-025s in April 1973, later followed by several Boeing 707-330Bs.

XT-ABX, Boeing 707-336C of Air Afrique, at Marseilles Airport on 4 July 1990. Ordered by BOAC-Cunard, and delivered on 19 December 1965 as G-ASZG, this aircraft subsequently passed to British Airways in April 1974, and was sold to TRATCO as LX-FCV in November 1983. It was re-registered as XT-ABX for Air Supply Corporation, then leased to Compagnie Nationale Naganagani, based in Burkina Faso, in September 1984. It was sub-leased to Air Afrique from July 1989 to May 1992. It was later flown to Southend, and was stored until August 1994, before being bought by Omega Air and registered as EL-AKI in November 1994. It was then leased to Brasair Transportes Aéreos (later known as BETA Cargo) as PP-BRB. The 707 was eventually withdrawn from use at Rio de Janeiro, and broken up in 1999.

CC-CEA, Boeing 707-330B operated by Lan-Chile, seen at Ezeiza Airport, Buenos Aires, on 15 November 1973. Originally delivered to Lufthansa in October 1965 as D-ABUC *Bremen*, this aircraft remained in service with the German carrier until March 1967, when it was bought by Lan-Chile as CC-CEA. It was then bought by the Chilean Air Force in June 1985, carrying serial FAC-903, and was converted to a Boeing 707-330C tanker in August 1996. It entered storage at Comodoro Arturo Merino Benitez Airport, Santiago, in February 2012.

5Y-AXI, Boeing 707-330B of African Airlines International, at Sharjah Airport, United Arab Emirates (UAE), on 9 November 1995. This 707 was delivered to Lufthansa and was in service with the airline from November 1965 to May 1982 as D-ABUF *Nürnberg*. It was bought by Air Zimbabwe in June 1982, as VP-WKV, and re-registered as Z-WKV in October 1983. It was then purchased by Seagreen Air Transport in October 1991, and sold to Kenyan operator African Airlines International in June 1993 as 5Y-AXI. African Airlines used the aircraft on a weekly passenger and cargo flight from Nairobi to Sharjah, UAE. It was withdrawn from use at Nairobi Airport in December 1999, and broken up in 2006.

D-ABUK, Boeing 707-330B of Lufthansa on approach to Schiphol Airport, Amsterdam, on 30 September 1978. This aircraft first flew on 18 March 1966, and was delivered to Lufthansa on 27 March 1966 as D-ABUK *Bochum*, remaining on the Lufthansa fleet until October 1980. It was sold to the United Arab Emirates government, as A6-UAE, in November 1980, and the UAE government then sold the 707 to Sudan Airways, as ST-NSR, in December 1986. It was used for spares to support the Sudan Airways 707 fleet, and was broken up at Khartoum Airport in 1995.

D-ABUA, Boeing 707-330C operated by German Cargo, seen at Nuremberg Airport in May 1979. German Cargo undertook freight charter services from Frankfurt Airport with three Boeing 707s. The carrier was a Lufthansa subsidiary, and began operations on 8 May 1977, ceasing operations on 1 May 1993. The aircraft pictured was delivered to Lufthansa in November 1965 as D-ABUA, but was leased to German Cargo. The aircraft has a long history, and was operated by a number of airlines, including Transcorp Airways, Ansett Air Freight, Global Air, Air Taxi International and Aries del Sur. Finally, it served with Ecuadorian carrier AECA Cargo as HC-BTB, before being stored and broken up at Guayaquil Airport, Ecuador, in 2000.

5N-MXX, Boeing 707-323C of Merchant Express Aviation, Nigeria, seen at Ostend Airport on 8 August 1997. This aircraft first served with American Airlines from August 1965 to April 1973 as N7561A. It was then bought by VARIG, as PP-VLP, in May 1973, and after 16 years of service with the Brazilian airline, it was sold to Aviation Leasing Group in June 1989. It was then leased to Buffalo Airways, Heavylift Cargo, Southeast Cargo and, in September 1994, Merchant Express. It was later stored at Southend Airport until 2000, before being leased to Ghana-based Johnsons Air as 9L-LAD in November 2000. It was withdrawn from use at Tripoli International Airport in October 2009.

JY-AEC, Boeing 707-384C of Alia Royal Jordanian Airlines, photographed at Schiphol Airport, Amsterdam, on 20 August 1989. This 707 was delivered to Olympic Airways in May 1966 as SX-DBB, staying with Olympic until February 1975, when it was sold to Alia Royal Jordanian Airlines as JY-AEC. It was then leased to Arab Air Cargo and Sierra Leone Airlines, returning to Alia Royal Jordanian in January 1987. It was later sold to the USAF to be used as the basis for a JSTARS (Joint Surveillance Target Attack Radar System) conversion, becoming Boeing E-8C, 93-0011. It was retired at Robins AFB, Georgia, and used as an E-8C instructional airframe, with age-related serial 66-30052, in February 2002.

SX-DBC, Boeing 707 of Olympic Airways, arriving at Schiphol Airport, Amsterdam, on 29 September 1969. Built for Olympic Airways, this aircraft first flew on 14 June 1966, and was delivered to Olympic on 18 June 1966 as SX-DBC *City of Knossos*. It remained in service with the Greek carrier for 24 years, and was sold to Israel Aircraft Industries (IAI) in March 1990 for conversion to a KC-137A tanker for the Fuerza Aerea Venezolana (Venezuelan Air Force). The KC-137A was delivered in January 1991, as FAV 8747, and was allocated to Escuadrón de Transportes T1, based at the El Libertador Air Base, near Maracay. It was placed in storage in 2008.

5A-DJS, Boeing 707-351C operated by Libyan carrier Jamahiriya Air Transport, seen at Schiphol Airport, Amsterdam, on 14 February 1985. Delivered to Northwest Orient Airlines on 15 November 1965, this 707 was bought by Cathay Pacific Airways as VR-HGQ in June 1973, and remained in service with Cathay until April 1982. The aircraft was then sold to Frespa AG in May 1982, before being sold on to Eagle Air (Iceland) as TF-VLP. It was leased to Libyan Arab Airlines in September 1982, as 5A-DJS, the airline merging with Jamahiriya Air Transport in June 1986. The aircraft was then sold to ZAS Airline of Egypt in November 1986 as 5Y-BFB.

D2-TOU, Boeing 707-351C operated by Angola Air Charter, seen at Manston Airport on 24 April 1992. Angola Air Charter was established in 1987, and is wholly owned by TAAG Angola Airlines, based at Quatro de Fevereiro Airport, Luanda. The company operated weekly cargo flights to Ostend Airport, Belgium. The aircraft was leased by Angola Air Charter from Equator Leasing Inc in December 1987, and later returned to the lease company before being flown to Manston Airport, on 12 June 1991, to be placed in storage. It was broken up in 2000.

9J-ADY, Boeing 707-349C of National Air Charters, at Schiphol Airport, Amsterdam, on 27 July 1985. Ordered by Flying Tiger Lines, and delivered on 13 October 1965 as N323F, this 707 was leased to Aer Lingus, as EI-ASN, from March 1969 to January 1973, and was then bought by Zambia Airways, as 9J-ADY, in March 1975. It was sold to National Air Charters in March 1985 and was bought by Trans Arabian Air Transport, as ST-ALK, in September 1988. The aircraft was damaged beyond repair at Khartoum Airport, Sudan, when the nose gear collapsed, damaging the nose and two engines.

ET-ABP, Boeing 720-060B of MEA (Middle East Airlines), seen at Brussels Airport, Zaventem, on 4 May 1969. This Boeing 720-060B, *Lalibela*, was wet-leased to Beirut-based MEA when planned expansion of Ethiopian Air Lines services had to be abandoned. Originally delivered to Ethiopian Air Lines as ET-ABP on 20 September 1965, the aircraft was leased to MEA from January 1966 to October 1969, and was then bought by AAR Corporation, as N400DS, in January 1988. It was stored at Mojave Airport, California, and broken up in October 2003.

FAC 904, Boeing 707-385C of the Fuerza Aérea de Chile (Chilean Air Force), at Schiphol Airport, Amsterdam, on 16 April 1991. This aircraft was initially operated by Boeing as N68657, and was sold to Lan-Chile on 20 December 1969 as CC-CEB. It was then bought by the Chilean Air Force, as FAC 905, in September 1991, and sent to Israel Aircraft Industries (IAI), Tel Aviv, in October 1994 for a Phalcon AEW (Airborne Early Warning) conversion. It returned to Chile as FAC 900, and was given the code FAC 904 in 1998, operating with Grupo 10 of the Fuerza Aérea de Chile. It was still operational in 2019.

RP-C1866, Aero Filipinas-liveried Boeing 707-351C, at Nagoya International Airport, Japan, on 15 August 1984. Originally delivered to Northwest Orient Airlines on 8 January 1966 as N364US, this aircraft was bought by Cathay Pacific Airways in November 1973, as VR-HGU, and remained in service with Cathay until November 1982. It was sold to Aero Filipinas as RP-C1866, and was then leased to Royal Nepal Airlines from November to December 1983, before being returned to Aero Filipinas. It was leased to Samoa Air from August 1984 to October 1985, before being bought by US-based Jetran in October 1985. It was later sold to Boeing for use in the KC-135 programme, and had been broken up by 2014.

N7096, Boeing 707-327C of TMA (Trans Mediterranean Airways) Cargo, Lebanon, pictured at Schiphol Airport, Amsterdam, on 16 February 1973. Ordered by Braniff Airways in May 1966 as N7096, this 707 was leased to TMA in March 1971, and after a successful lease, TMA bought the aircraft in July 1980 as OD-AGY. It was then leased to Kuwait Airlines and Air Afrique, before returning to TMA. It was withdrawn from use at Beirut Airport, featuring an all-white colour scheme, in February 2002, and was probably broken up later that year.

LX-LGU, Boeing 707-344B of Luxair, at Luxembourg Airport on 29 July 1978. This 707 was ordered by South African Airways, and delivered on 9 January 1967 as ZS-EKV *Windhoek*. It was sold to Luxair as LX-LGU, and remained in service with the operator from July 1977 to April 1983. It was then bought by Air Mauritius, as 3B-NAF, before passing through a succession of operators, including Club Air, African Express Airways (as 5Y-AXS), Air Atlanta Icelandic, Lennox Airlines (as 5Y-LKL) and Omega Air (as N6598W). It was sold to Boeing in October 1990, and stored at Davis-Monthan AFB before being broken up.

OO-SJJ, Boeing 707-329C of Sabena, at Brussels Airport, Zaventem, on 19 June 1979. Delivered to Sabena on 23 March 1966 as OO-SJJ, this 707 left the Belgian airline's fleet after 17 years, and was sold to Katale Aero Transport, Zaire, as 9Q-CVG in July 1983. The aircraft was damaged beyond repair during a heavy landing at Goma Airport, Zaire, on 1 March 1990. Sabena was formed on 23 May 1923, providing comprehensive European services together with a worldwide route network to cities including Anchorage, Mexico City, Manila, Conakry and Douala. The airline ceased operations on 7 November 2001.

S2-ABN, Boeing 707-351C operated by Bangladesh Biman, photographed at Schiphol Airport, Amsterdam, on 19 February 1983. Originally delivered to Northwest Orient Airlines as N367US in July 1966, this aircraft was bought by Bangladesh Biman on 12 December 1973, as S2-ABN *Land of Shah Jalal*, and was sold to Fast Cargo Airways (Iceland) in June 1988. It was then leased to Nigerian operator GAS Air as 5N-AYJ. During a flight from Dar es Salaam, via Cairo, to Brussels, it made several approaches at Cairo International Airport, but because of bad weather it was diverted to Luxor Airport. The aircraft never made it to Luxor, as it ran out of fuel and crashed at Karam Omram, near Luxor.

YA-GAF, Boeing 707-324C of Uganda Airlines, pictured at Ostend Airport on 7 June 1997. Delivered to Continental Air Lines in June 1966 as N17325, this aircraft was bought by VARIG, as PP-VLN, in April 1973, and remained with the Brazilian carrier until September 1989. It was sold to the Aviation Leasing Group, as N110BV, in October 1989, and was subsequently leased to Buffalo Airways, Heavylift and Uganda Airlines (as 5X-UCM). The aircraft was seized by the Yugoslav Air Force in August 1991, and flown to Nis Airport, Serbia, for storage. It was bought by Balkh Airlines (Afghanistan) in January 1997, as YA-GAF, then leased to Uganda Airlines, before being stored and broken up at Ostend Airport in December 1998.

9L-LDU, Boeing 707-373C of Sierra Leone-based Koda Air Cargo, seen at Sabiha Gökçen Airport, Istanbul, on 25 March 2006. Originally delivered to World Airways as N372WA in May 1966, this aircraft was bought by Portuguese carrier TAP in July 1974, as CS-TBJ, the airline changing its name to TAP Air Portugal in April 1979. The 707 was then sold to Sicotra Aviation, as 9Q-CSB, in December 1987, before passing through several operators, including Skydec Cargo and Tradewinds Air Cargo (as 3C-CSB). It was bought by Koda Air Cargo in April 2001, and then sold to Air Leone in November 2003 as 9L-LDU. The aircraft was loaded with textile materials on 26 December 2005, and caught fire while parked on the apron at Sabiha Gökçen Airport, Istanbul. It was broken up in 2019.

CX-BJV, Boeing 707-331C of Aero Uruguay, at Miami International Airport on 19 November 1980. Aero Uruguay provided cargo charter services between Uruguay and Europe, and throughout North, Central and South America, including flights to Luxembourg and New York. The company was formed by Cargolux, and began operations on 12 November 1977 with a flight from Montevideo to San Juan, using a Canadair CL-44D4-2 freighter. The company's first jet, the 707-331C pictured here, arrived in October 1978 as LX-FCV, before being re-registered as CX-BJV. Aero Uruguay ceased operations in 2005.

9G-ACY, Boeing 707-331C of West Coast Airlines, at Schiphol Airport, Amsterdam, on 15 December 1984. Delivered to Trans World Airlines as N5771T in June 1967, this aircraft was sold to Guinness Peat Aviation in May 1978 as EI-BER. It was leased to Aer Lingus, Cargolux and, in October 1978, to Aero Uruguay as CX-BJV. It returned to Cargolux in August 1981, and then passed through a number of operators, including Zimex Aviation, West Coast Airlines, Transcorp Airways, Omega Air, Southern Air Transport, Millon Air and Jetlease. The aircraft's final operator was Florida West, which operated the 707 as N730FW, before it was stored at Miami and broken up during 1995.

N730FW, Boeing 707-331C of Florida West Airlines, pictured at Asunción International Airport, Paraguay, on 15 November 1988. Florida West Airlines was established in 1981, based at Miami International Airport, operating scheduled cargo flights worldwide. After being declared bankrupt in October 1994, the airline's assets were sold to Florida West International Airways, and operations recommenced in March 1996, with a large fleet of Boeing 707s, Boeing 767s and Douglas DC8s. Florida West International Airways ceased operations in February 2017.

OD-AGS, Boeing 707-331C of Kuwait Airways Cargo, photographed at Schiphol Airport, Amsterdam, on 21 February 1994. Originally ordered by Trans World Airlines, and delivered in September 1967 as N5773T, this aircraft was leased to Golden Sun Air Cargo from December 1971 to March 1972, then sold to TMA (Trans Mediterranean Airways), as OD-AGS, in March 1978. TMA leased the 707 to Kuwait Airways Cargo from June 1991 to December 1997, and it was then stored at Beirut in 2001, and broken up in 2011. Kuwait National Airways was formed in 1953, and the name Kuwait Airways was adopted in May 1958. The airline ordered three new Boeing 707-369Cs in 1967, which were delivered in November 1968.

CX-BNU, Boeing 707-387B leased by PLUNA (Uruguay), at Rio de Janeiro International Airport on 24 October 1988. Originally ordered by Aerolíneas Argentinas, this 707 first flew on 5 December 1966, and was delivered on 16 December 1966 as LV-ISB *Almilan*. It remained in service with the Argentine airline until it was leased to PLUNA (Primeras Líneas Uruguayas de Navegación Aérea), as CX-BNU, in May 1981. PLUNA bought the aircraft in December 1988, and it was then leased to LADE (Argentina) and Fly Linhas Aéreas (Brazil), as PP-LBN, returning to PLUNA in February 1996. It was bought by the Brazilian Air Force (FAB – Força Aérea Brasileira) in August 1996, and was used for spare parts for the FAB 707 fleet, before being broken up at Rio de Janeiro during 1997.

LV-ISD, Boeing 707-387B of Aerolíneas Argentinas, pictured at Jorge Chavez Airport, Lima, on 2 November 1977. This aircraft was originally delivered to Aerolíneas Argentinas and served with the airline from February 1967 to December 1982 as LV-ISD *Procion*. It was then sold to the Fuerza Aérea Argentina (Argentine Air Force), as TC-95, on 18 January 1983, and re-coded as T-95. It was leased to PLUNA (Uruguay) for several months in 1988 as LV-ISD, then returned to Argentina as T-95. It was stored at El Palomar Air Base in June 2004, and was broken up in 2015. Aerolíneas Argentinas was formed in May 1949, when the Ministry of Transport took over the activities of all the smaller airlines in Argentina, with the exception of the Air Force-controlled LADE (Líneas Aéreas del Estado).

N448M, Boeing 707-321C of Maverick International, at Schiphol Airport, Amsterdam, on 5 May 1978. Originally delivered to Pan American World Airways as N448PA *Clipper Pacific Raider*, in May 1967, this 707 was bought by US leasing company ATASCO in September 1977, and leased to Maverick in October 1977. It was re-registered as N448M in May 1978. It then passed through a succession of operators, including British Midland, Pakistan International Airlines (PIA), Zaire Aero Services (ZAS), Gulf Air, Air Rwanda, Eagle Air, Libyan Arab Airlines, Burlington Express, Aero USA, Florida West and Air Atlantic (as 5N-EEO). It was later stored at Lagos Airport in Nigeria, and was broken up in 2002.

N448M, Boeing 707-321C of Zaire Aero Service, at Schiphol Airport, Amsterdam, on 23 September 1979. This aircraft is also pictured previously in its Maverick International livery. Zaire Aero Service (ZAS) was based at N'Djili International Airport, near Kinshasa. Little is known about the history of ZAS, but the company operated predominantly cargo services, and between 1976 and 1978 it had a large fleet of propliners and turbo-props, including Douglas DC-4s and DC-6As, a Bristol Britannia, Vickers Viscount and Fokker F27-600. ZAS leased N448M in 1979 from ATASCO Leasing, originally still carrying the livery of the previous operator, Pakistan International Airlines.

YR-ABM, Boeing 707-321C of Romanian carrier TAROM (Transporturi Aeriene Române), at Ostend Airport on 24 April 1992. TAROM was founded in 1946, as a joint Romanian-Soviet company, under the title of Transporturi Aeriene Române Sovietica (TARS). In 1954, the company's Soviet share was purchased by the Romanian government, and by 1960 the airline was flying to many European destinations. The first TAROM flight to New York with a 707, via Amsterdam, took place in 1966. This aircraft was originally delivered to Pan American World Airways in May 1967 as N450PA. It was bought by TAROM in August 1975, and was later leased to Air Zaire and Air Afrique. It was written off on 15 January 1993, at Abidjan Airport (Ivory Coast), when the 707 undershot the runway after an instrument approach, causing the main undercarriage to collapse.

F-BLCE, Boeing 707-328B of Air France, at Bordeaux-Mérignac Airport on 2 December 1972. Delivered to Air France on 7 March 1967 as F-BLCE *Chateau D'Usse*, this 707 was leased to Air Afrique as TU-TXL. It was then leased by Air Guinée, and bought by the airline in July 1981 as 3X-GCC. It was later sold to Trans European Airways (TEA) as OO-TYC, operating with the Belgian airline from May 1984 to January 1989. It entered storage at Brussels Airport, Zaventem, and was then registered as N2090B to Commodore Aviation, before being bought by Israel Aircraft Industries (IAI) in July 1989. It was transferred to IAI as 4X-BYC in July 1990, and converted to ELINT (Electronic Intelligence) specification in August 1990. It was observed withdrawn from use at Tel Aviv in 2001.

9XR-JA, Boeing 707-328C of Air Rwanda, seen at Schiphol Airport, Amsterdam, on 22 July 1984. This aircraft first flew on 25 February 1967, and was originally ordered by Air France, serving with the airline from 15 March 1967 to June 1979. It was bought by Air Rwanda in July 1979, as 9XR-JA, and was re-registered as 9XR-VO in June 1995. Air Rwanda was founded by the government of Rwanda on 15 July 1975, and was rebranded Rwanda Air in 1996. This was the only 707 operated by the airline, and in April 1996 the aircraft was bought by Espace Aviation as P4-ESP. It was flown to Manston Airport in October 1998, and was broken up during 2000. (Peter de Groot)

G-BFLE, Boeing 707-338C of Air Algerie, at East Midlands Airport in June 1979. This 707 first flew on 9 December 1966, and served with Qantas from 28 January 1967 to May 1978 as VH-EBT. It was then bought by the Itel Air leasing company, as G-BFLE, and was leased to numerous airlines, including British Midland, Pakistan International Airlines, Air Algérie, Gulf Air, DETA Mozambique, Ariana Afghan and LAM Mozambique. It was bought by ATASCO Leasing in August 1985, and leased to Burlington Express, Aero USA and Buffalo Airways. It was then sold to Northrop Grumman Corporation and converted to Boeing E-8C JSTARS (Joint Surveillance Target Attack Radar System) specification, as 94-0284, for the USAF.

N107BV, Boeing 707-341C of Buffalo Airways, pictured at Waco Regional Airport on 2 April 1992. Delivered to VARIG in December 1966 as PP-VJS, this aircraft was leased to Transbrasil from September 1982 to November 1984, and was then sold to Aviation Leasing Group as N107BV. It was leased to Buffalo Airways from May 1989 to May 1994, but was also sub-leased to Malev (Hungary) in 1990–91. Norske Finance then bought the 707, and it was leased to Azerbaijan Airlines, as 4K-AZ3, in June 1994. It was transferred to Azerbaijan Airlines Cargo in December 1997, and later stored at Southend Airport, before being broken up in February 2002.

9V-BEY, Boeing 707-324C of Singapore Airlines, at Schiphol Airport, Amsterdam, on 22 May 1973. In a rare sight, this Boeing 707-324C is fitted with a 'Pod-Pak' – an aerodynamically shaped nacelle used to transport a spare engine, or an engine requiring maintenance, under the wing. Nine major airlines flying 707s ordered Pod-Paks. Delivered to Continental Airlines in May 1967 as N47330, this aircraft was then sold to Singapore Airlines as 9V-BEY, and was operated by the airline from 1 October 1972 to November 1981. The aircraft later passed through a considerable number of other operators, including Arrow Air, Shanghai Airlines, Comtran International, Florida West, Royal Jordanian, Amed Air, Jason Air and Nigeria Airways. Finally, it was stored at Lagos Airport, and broken up in 2002.

ST-AMF, Boeing 707-321C of Trans Arabian Air Transport, at Ostend Airport on 7 June 1997. Originally delivered to Pan American World Airways as N457PA, in October 1967, this aircraft was bought by ATASCO Leasing in June 1978, and leased to Pelican Air Transport as G-BPAT. It returned to ATASCO a year later, and was bought by Zambia Airways, as 9J-AEQ, in June 1979. It was then sold to TAAT (Trans Arabian Air Transport – Sudan) in February 1989 as ST-ALM. Next, it was leased to Air Hong Kong from May 1989 to October 1992, as VR-HKL, and was returned to TAAT before entering storage at Khartoum in 2003.

F-BYCO, Boeing 707-321C operated by Air France Cargo, at Anchorage Airport on 17 April 1980. Air France began jet operations in 1960, with Sud Aviation SE 210 Caravelles and Boeing 707s, initially using three Caravelles and three 707s. It was a revolution, flying to New York from Paris in just eight hours, compared with 14 hours using a Super Constellation. Bought by Pan American World Airways as N463PA in December 1967, this aircraft was sold to Air France in October 1975 as F-BYCO, leaving the airline's fleet in June 1975. It then served with a number of other operators, including Pan Aviation, World Airline Gambia, Sud Americana Peru and Millon Air (as N722GS). It was placed in storage at Miami, and broken up in 1999.

HK-2473X, Boeing 707-321C of Avianca (Colombia), at El Dorado Airport, Bogotá, on 17 November 1980. Ordered by Pan American World Airways, and delivered in January 1968 as N473PA, this 707 was later sold to Ronair and leased to Iran Air in October 1978 as N473RN. It then had a long history, passing through a large number of operators, including Transcarga (Venezuela), Avianca, Faucett (Peru), Radix Air, Burlington Air Express, Aero USA, Omega Air, Shabair, Brasair, Skymaster Airlines and, finally, Omega Air in August 1998. It was flown to Southend, as N2NF, in 1999 and was later damaged by arson. It was broken up during 2007.

OO-PSI, Boeing 707-321B in Sobelair livery, at Brussels Airport, Zaventem, in March 1979. Sobelair was founded on 30 July 1946 as a charter company, and began operations between Belgium and the Congo that same year. In 1947, the company established a scheduled feeder network within Congo, to supplement the main service operated by Sabena. The company ceased operations on 19 January 2004. Originally delivered to Pan American World Airways, as N455PA, on 6 February 1968, this aircraft was sold to Compagnie European Recherches, as OO-PSI, in January 1979. It was then leased to Sobelair for two years, before being bought by United African Airlines in September 1981 as 5A-DJM. A few months later it was sold to Libyan Arab Airlines, and stored at Cairo. It was broken up in 2009. (Michel Anciaux)

OO-PSI, Boeing 707-321B cockpit at Brussels Airport, Zaventem, in March 1979. The computer-controlled glass-cockpit screens of today were still years away when the 707s came on the scene. Here, we see the cockpit of the Sobelair 707 pictured previously, which was originally delivered to Pan American in February 1968. The pilot's and co-pilot's seats are visible, along with the controls and systems they had to monitor. The co-pilot's seat could rotate from a rear-facing to front-facing position, to enable him to assist the pilot with the engine controls during the take-off and landing phases of flight. A jump-seat was provided for an extra pilot on long flights. (Michel Anciaux)

9Y-TEE, Boeing 707-351C of BWIA (British West Indian Airways), pictured at London Heathrow Airport on 16 October 1977. Boarding at London Heathrow, this photograph shows flight BW900, on which the author flew to Port of Spain, Trinidad, which took 8hrs 45min by BWIA Boeing 707-351C. First flown on 7 March 1967, and delivered to Northwest Orient Airlines on 18 March 1967, this 707 was bought by BWIA in July 1974, and was operated as 9Y-TEE *Humming Bird*. It was sold in February 1981, to Caribbean Air Cargo as 8P-CAC. It subsequently saw service with a number of airlines, including Dynair, Skyways International and Florida West Airlines. It was bought by TAAT (Trans Arabian Air Transport – Sudan) in April 1998, and operated as ST-APY. During a flight from Khartoum to Mwanza, Tanzania, on 3 February 2000, the aircraft crashed on landing at Mwanza, and ended up in Lake Victoria.

9G-OOD, Boeing 707-399C of FIA (First International Airways), seen at Sharjah Airport, United Arab Emirates, on 12 November 2000. Originally delivered to Caledonian Airways in July 1967 as G-AVKA *County of Ayr*, this 707 was leased to Flying Tiger Line for almost a year, and returned to Caledonian in June 1968. It was bought by TAP as CS-TBH in May 1973, and remained in service with the Portuguese carrier until October 1983. It subsequently passed through many leasing companies and airlines, such as Buffalo Airways, Azerbaijan Airlines, First International Airways, Air Cargo Plus, Kinshasa Airways and, in July 2006, Etram Air Wing, Angola (as D2-FDZ). It was later stored at Luanda Airport, Angola, and broken up June 2012.

N525EJ, Boeing 707-355C of Air Bahama, seen at Paris Le Bourget Airport in May 1969. Delivered to Executive Jet Aviation in May 1967 as N525EJ, this aircraft was leased by Air Bahama from June 1968 to October 1969. It was then leased to World Airlift, and sub-leased to Caledonian Airways, as G-AYEX, from June 1970 to March 1973. Subsequently, it was bought by Aviation Consultants, and leased to Saint Lucia Airways, Keyway Air Transport, HCL Aviation and E-Systems. Finally, it was bought by the USAF, and converted to an EC-137D, 64-19417, for AFSOC (Air Force Special Operations Command), before entering storage at Davis-Monthan AFB in June 2002.

PP-VLI, Boeing 707-385C of VARIG Cargo, at Miami International Airport on 20 November 1980. Originally sold to American Airlines on 6 December 1966 as N8400, this aircraft was then bought by VARIG, as PP-VLI, in September 1971. It was then then sold to the Aviation Leasing Group, as N109BV, in May 1989 and leased to Buffalo Airways until July 1989. Ethiopian Airlines bought the aircraft from the leasing company, as ET-AJZ, in October 1990. It was destroyed on 25 March 1991 at Asmara International Airport, Eritrea, when shelled by rebels during loading.

9G-ACX, Boeing 707-336C of West Africa Airline Cargo, pictured at Schiphol Airport, Amsterdam, on 15 February 1983. Ordered by BOAC, and delivered on 30 November 1967 as G-ATWV, this 707 was transferred to British Airways in April 1974, when the two companies merged. It was bought by Clipper International in January 1981, and leased to West Africa Airline in February 1982. It was returned in April 1986, and was then leased to Saint Lucia Airways, Caribbean Air Transport, Seagreen Air Transport, Grecoair and Aero Zambia (as 5Y-BNJ). It was stored at Polokwane Airport, South Africa, in January 2004, and broken up in 2016.

ZS-IJI, Boeing 707-323C operated by Interair, photographed at Polokwane Airport, South Africa, on 14 November 2003. Delivered to American Airlines on 28 August 1967 as N7597A, this aircraft was sold to American Trans Air (ATA) in September 1982, and subsequently operated by Transbrasil (as PT-TCL), Omega Air, Israel Aircraft Industries (as 4X-AOY), Lesotho Airways (as 7P-LAN) and Seagreen Air Transport (as N29AZ). The 707 was later leased by Lan-Chile (as CC-CDI) and Aero Zambia, and was bought by Inter Air (as ZS-IJI) in January 2000. It was stored at Polokwane Airport, and was broken up in August 2016.

HS-TFS, Boeing 707-323C of Thai Flying Cargo, at Sharjah Airport, United Arab Emirates, on 13 November 2000. This aircraft first flew on 27 August 1967, and was delivered to American Airlines as N7599A on 11 September 1967. It was sold 16 years later to American Trans Air (ATA), which then sold the 707 to Transbrasil as PT-TCK in February 1985. It then passed through a number of operators, including Air Swazi Cargo, Omega Air, Safair, Express Cargo, Air Cess, Inter African Cargo Airlines, Air Ghana, and finally, Thai Flying Cargo. The aircraft was then stored at U-Tapao Airport, Thailand, and bought by Equaflight, as TN-AGO, in October 2000. It was damaged beyond repair on 7 September 2001, when the landing gear collapsed at Lubumbashi Airport, Democratic Republic of Congo.

HB-IEI, Boeing 707-328C of Homac Aviation, at Manston Airport on 24 April 1992. This aircraft served with its first operator, Air France, from 3 June 1967 to March 1983, as F-BLCG, and was then sold to ZAS Airline of Egypt, as SU-DAB, on 29 March 1983. It was later leased to Nile Safari Aviation until July 1986, before passing through a number of operators, including Naganagani (Burkina Faso), Homac Aviation (Switzerland), Tradewinds Airways, Yana Air Cargo (Kenya), Avistar (Cyprus), Azerbaijan Airlines and Clipper International (as 9G-ROX). The 707 left Bratislava for N'Djamena (Chad) on 7 February 1999, and during take-off numbers two and three engines failed. The take-off was aborted, but the aircraft overran the runway, sustaining damage, and was subsequently scrapped.

9V-BDC, Boeing 707-327C of MSA (Malaysia-Singapore Airlines), at Kai Tak Airport, Hong Kong, on 24 March 1972. MSA was formed on 30 December 1966, and its services were subsequently taken over by Singapore Airlines (SIA), which was established as the national airline of Singapore in January 1972. This 707 was originally delivered to Braniff Airways, as N7103, on 18 October 1967, and was bought by MSA in April 1971. It was sold to International Air Leases as N707ME, and served with Shanghai Airlines (as B-2424), Ladeco (Chile – as CC-CYA), and Jaro International (Romania – as YR-JCA). The aircraft was withdrawn from service in 1997, and broken up at Bucharest Airport in 2004.

ET-AIV, Boeing 707-327C operated by Ethiopian Cargo, pictured at Bole International Airport, Addis Ababa, on 21 January 1988. This aircraft first flew on 8 November 1967, and was delivered to Braniff International on 20 November 1967 as N7104. It was leased to TMA (Trans Mediterranean Airways), as N7104, from August 1973 to September 1980 and then bought by the airline on 5 September 1980, re-registered as OD-AGZ. After five years of service, TMA sold the 707 to Ethiopian Airlines Cargo as ET-AIV in May 1985. The aircraft was then sold to the government of the Democratic Republic of Congo, as 9Q-CGC, on 26 November 1998. In April 2000, during a major fire at N'Djili Airport, Kinshasa, several aircraft, including this one, were destroyed.

N15710, Boeing 707-331C of Aerotal Colombia, at Miami Airport on 20 November 1980. Delivered to Trans World Airlines on 26 June 1968 as N15710, this aircraft was bought by Guinness Peat Aviation in March 1979, and sub-leased to Cargolux, Faucett, and to Aerotal Colombia in December 1979. It was returned to Guinness Peat in November 1980, and flown to Marana Pinal Air Park, Arizona, for storage in 1983. It was then bought by Boeing and transferred in January 1985 to the USAF, as 84-1399, to be converted to a TC-18E for use as an AWACS (Airborne Warning And Control System) trainer. It was later stored at Tinker AFB, Oklahoma, and broken up in 2002.

N7231T, Boeing 707-331B of Atlanta Skylarks, at Schiphol Airport, Amsterdam, on 23 June 1984. This 707 first flew on 11 March 1968, and was delivered to Trans World Airlines on 22 March 1968 as N28727. It was then leased to Aramco (Saudi Arabia), and returned to TWA in June 1980. It was subsequently sold to Independent Air in August 1983, and was leased to Atlanta Skylarks, as N7231T, in September 1983. The aircraft was later returned to Independent Air. On 8 February 1989, during a flight from Bergamo (Italy) via Santa Maria (Azores) to Punta Cana (Dominican Republic), as the 707 approached Santa Maria Airport, it collided with a rock wall on the side of a road near the top of the Pico Alto mountain (586m/1,900ft). There were no survivors.

N8412, Boeing 707-323C of American Airlines, seen at San Juan Airport, Puerto Rico, on 2 October 1979. American Airlines owes its origins to American Airways, which was formed in 1930 and contributed heavily to determining the specification of several famous aircraft, such as the DC-3, DC-7, Convair 240, 880 and 990, and latterly the Boeing 707 and 720. N8412 was ordered by American Airlines in June 1968, and was leased to Aerotal Colombia, as HK-2842X, in June 1982. It was bought by Israel Aircraft Industries in March 1985, and was modified as a KC-137C for the Peruvian Air Force (FAP-319), which was delivered in February 1988. It was withdrawn from use in 2003.

N8414, Boeing 707-323C of MME Farms Maintenance Corporation, at London Stansted Airport on 15 August 1984. This aircraft first flew on 13 June 1968, and was operated by American Airlines from 26 June 1968 to October 1980 as N8414. It was bought by Western Co, and sold to MME in August 1982. It then passed through a number of operators, including Jet East International, Safair, Shabair (Zaire) and Zaire Airlines as 9Q-CKK. Zaire Airlines later became Congo Airlines. On 1 November 1997, the aircraft was damaged beyond repair when it landed with the nose gear retracted. It was later used for spares for other 707s at Kinshasa Airport.

N751MA, Boeing 707-323C of Millon Air, seen at Miami International Airport on 20 November 1990. Originally delivered to American Airlines, as N8402, in October 1967, this 707 was bought by Nautilus Sportwear Medical Industries in February 1984, and then sold to Challenge Air Cargo in June 1986. It was later operated by several lease companies and airlines, such as Transway Air International, Regent Air and Millon Air. On 22 October 1996, N751MA was operating on a flight from Manta, Ecuador, to Miami, when it crashed shortly after take-off. The 707 damaged the rooftops of houses near the airport, and crashed in flames. Local officials claimed an engine was on fire.

P2-ANB, Boeing 707-338C of Air Niugini, at Brussels Airport, Zaventem, in February 1985. Air Niugini was formed in 1973 as the national airline of Papua New Guinea. Operations commenced on 1 November 1973, using a large fleet of Fokker F27s, with two leased 707s arriving in 1976–77. The airline operated scheduled passenger services and cargo flights on domestic and international routes. Delivered to Qantas, as VH-EAA, on 8 December 1967, this aircraft was bought by Young Cargo, as OO-YCK, in May 1977 and then sold to Air Niugini in December 1984. It also served with several other airlines, including Air Arctic Iceland, Kenya Airways, Air Maldives and ZAS Airline of Egypt. It was acquired by Northrop Grumman Corporation in June 1990, and converted to an E-8C JSTARS (Joint Surveillance Target Attack Radar System), as 90-0175, for the USAF.

OO-YCL, Boeing 707-338C of Young Cargo, at Ostend Airport on 16 January 1978. Young Cargo was formed on 9 September 1974, to operate cargo charter services on a worldwide basis. The airline's first revenue-earning flight took place on 4 March 1975, from Milan to Stavanger, using a swing-tail Canadair CL-44, leased from Cargolux. Young Cargo then operated a fleet of four Bristol Britannias, and two Boeing 707s joined the fleet in 1977. Delivered to Qantas in January 1968 as VH-EAB, this aircraft was sold to Young Cargo, as OO-YCL, on 28 December 1977. Over the years, it also served with Air Niugini, Air Arctic Iceland, Surinam Airways, ZAS, Nile Safari Aviation and Avistar. In May 1992, it was bought by Northrop Grumman Corporation, and was converted to an E-8C JSTARS (Joint Surveillance Target Attack Radar System), as 90-3289, for the USAF.

SU-DAE, Boeing 707-338C operated by ZAS Airline of Egypt, at Schiphol Airport, Amsterdam, on 15 February 1988. ZAS Airline of Egypt was formed by two brothers, Emir and Sherif Zarkani. Operations began on 23 November 1982, with cargo flights from Cairo to Amsterdam and London, mainly carrying fresh fruits and vegetables. The company's main operating base was Schiphol Airport, Amsterdam. ZAS also based Lockheed L-1329 JetStars at Amsterdam for the business market. SU-DAE was bought by ZAS from TRATCO leasing in February 1986. It was originally delivered to Qantas, as VH-EAB, in 1986. ZAS Airline of Egypt ceased operations in April 1995.

5N-BBD, Boeing 707-338C of ADC Airlines, at Ostend Airport on 7 June 1997. In 1990, Nigerian Aviation Development Company set up ADC Airlines, and received its license to operate scheduled passenger and cargo services. ADC Airlines commenced flight operations on 1 January 1991, and at the height of its operations, in 1996, it had seven aircraft – three Boeing 727s, three BAC 1-11s and one Boeing 707 for cargo flights to Europe. The company ceased operations in April 2007. Delivered to Qantas, as VH-EAE, in April 1968, this 707 served with many airlines, such as British Midland Airways, DETA Mozambique, Burlington Express, Aero USA, and finally, from April 1994, ADC. The aircraft was flown to Manston Airport in August 1997, and broken up in 2001.

9Y-TEJ, Boeing 707-351C of BWIA International, at Miami Airport on 28 November 1981. BWIA (British West Indian Airways) was founded on 27 November 1939 by Lowell Yerex. The company began operations on 17 November 1940, with a Lockheed Lodestar, flying between Caribbean countries. From 1967, BWIA was owned by the government of Trinidad, flying scheduled passenger services to San Juan (Puerto Rico), Caracas, Miami, New York, Toronto, Kingston (Jamaica) and Georgetown (Guyana). The London route was first flown in 1975, with 9Y-TEJ, which was bought from Northwest Orient Airlines in January 1975. BWIA ceased operations in 2006.

N2215Y, Boeing 707-351C operated by Jet Freight Pacific, photographed at Barajas Airport, Madrid, on 29 September 1988. Originally delivered to Northwest Orient Airlines on 14 October 1967 as N375US, this aircraft was bought by BWIA (British West Indian Airways), as 9Y-TEJ, in January 1975. It served with BWIA for eight years, and was sold to Aviation Technical Support in January 1981. It then passed through several lease companies and airlines, including Eagle Aviation, Westar International, Exec Air, Jetran, Skystar, Universal Airways, Buffalo Airways, and Jet Freight Pacific. Finally, it was leased to Overnight Cargo, as 5N-OCL, until October 1994. From September 1995, it was stored (as N2215Y) at Smyrna Airport, Tennessee, and was broken up in 1997.

N376US, Boeing 707-351C of Northwest Airlines, at Kai Tak Airport, Hong Kong, on 24 April 1972. Northwest Airlines, trading as Northwest Orient Airlines, was established on 1 August 1926 as Northwest Airways Inc, and it was awarded a mail contract covering the route from Chicago to Minneapolis St. Paul. Transcontinental routes were flown from 1 June 1945, with services to New York and Tokyo flying the 'Great Circle' route, via Alaska. Delivered to Northwest Orient in November 1967 as N376US, this aircraft remained in service with the carrier until 1975, when it was sold to BWIA (British West Indian Airways) as 9Y-TEK. It flew with a number of other airlines, including Caribbean Air Cargo, Skyways and Trans Arabian Air Transport (as ST-ANP). On 14 August 1999, it overran the runway at Juba Airport, South Sudan, and was damaged beyond repair.

5N-AOQ, Boeing 707-355C of Okada Air, at Schiphol Airport, Amsterdam, on 5 June 1985. Okada Air was formed in 1983, based at Benin, Nigeria. The company began operations in 1984, with a fleet of BAC 1-11-300s, and a Boeing 707 was acquired for cargo operations in July 1984. This aircraft was delivered to Executive Jet Aviation, as N526EJ, during November 1967 and was leased to Transavia Holland, as PH-TRF, from May 1968 to October 1968. The next operator was Caledonian Airways (as G-AXRS), followed by Monarch, Okada Air, Eagle Air and Peak Aviation. The 707 was returned to Okada Air in October 1994, and leased to International Air Tours in October 1996 as 5N-VRG. During a flight from Ostend Airport to Lagos, on 14 November 1998, it returned to Ostend and overshot the runway, sustaining damage that resulted in a write-off.

CC-CEJ, Boeing 707-321B of Lan-Chile, pictured at Miami Airport on 20 November 1980. Originally delivered to Pan American World Airways on 8 December 1968 as N491PA, this 707 was sold to ATASCO Leasing in October 1979, and leased to Lan-Chile, as CC-CEJ, from December 1979 to September 1981. The aircraft was then leased to Faucett and Guyana Airways, before entering storage at Marana Pinal Air Park, Arizona, in December 1984. It was bought by Boeing, as N1181Z, in February 1986 and used for the KC-135 programme, eventually being broken up at Davis-Monthan AFB in 2013.

ZS-SAF, Boeing 707-344C of South African Airways, at Johannesburg Airport in June 1975. Delivered to South African Airways, as ZS-EUX, in April 1968, this aircraft was re-registered as ZS-SAF in December 1968. It was bought by Luxair, as LX-LGT, on 14 July 1978 and leased to Sabena, Cargolux, Luxavia, Royal Jordanian Airlines, Eagle Air, Safair and Air Swazi Cargo. It was then stored at Tel Aviv, before being converted to ELINT (Electronic Intelligence) specification for the South African Air Force (SAAF) in May 1995. It served with the SAAF, as 1423, until it was withdrawn from use in 2007, and used for spares at Waterkloof Air Force Base. The aircraft's final flight, on 10 July 2007, took it to Bujumbura (Burundi), Kinshasa and Kindu (Democratic Republic of Congo).

G-AVTW, Boeing 707-399C of Caledonian Airways, seen at Schiphol Airport, Amsterdam on 7 February 1971. Originally ordered by Caledonian Airways, as G-AVTW, and delivered on 29 December 1967, this aircraft was leased by BOAC, which merged with British United Airways in November 1970. It was then bought by Portuguese carrier TAP, as CS-TBI, in April 1973, before being leased to Nigeria Airways for two months. It returned to TAP, and was leased to Dominicana (Dominican Republic) in November 1983 as HI-442. Dominicana bought the 707 in July 1984, as HI-442CT, and ran scheduled services from Santo Domingo to San Juan (Puerto Rico), Curaçao, Miami and New York. The aircraft was placed into storage in 1992, and broken up at Santo Domingo Airport in 2009.

SU-AOU, Boeing 707-366C operated by Egyptair, at Hellinikon Airport, Athens, on 6 April 1973. Delivered to United Arab Airlines (renamed Egyptair on 10 October 1971), as SU-AOU, in September 1968, this 707 was in service with the Egyptian airline until February 1994. It was acquired by New ACS, as 9Q-CJM, and re-registered as 9Q-CRA in November 1994. It was then sold to Zaire Express, as 9Q-CKG, in November 1995, before being transferred to Hewa Bora Airways (Democratic Republic of Congo) in July 1998, and registered in 2002 as 9Q-CKB. On a flight from Johannesburg to N'Djili, Kinshasa, the weather was stormy on arrival, and directional control was lost during landing, causing the 707 to veer off the runway. This resulted in the right-hand main undercarriage collapsing. The aircraft was damaged beyond repair.

SU-PBB, Boeing 707-328C in Air Memphis livery, at Ostend Airport on 7 June 1997. This aircraft first flew in November 1968, and served with Air France from 4 December 1968 to October 1982 as F-BLCK *Chateau de Langeais*. It was sold to ZAS Airline of Egypt, as SU-DAA, on 12 November 1982 and remained in service with ZAS until October 1996, when it was sold to Air Memphis as SU-PBB. The 707 was then stored at Cairo International Airport from June 2002, and was broken up in 2003. Air Memphis was a charter airline founded in 1996, operating passenger and cargo flights from Egypt to several European destinations. It ceased operations in 2013.

C5-MBM, Boeing 707-347C of Bin Mahfooz Aviation, seen at Bole International Airport, Addis Ababa, on 22 April 2005. Ordered by Western Airlines, this 707 first flew on 30 August 1968, and was delivered on 10 September 1968 as N1504W. After 12 years in service with Western Airlines, it was sold to MEA (Middle East Airlines), as OD-AGU, in May 1980. It was then leased to Espace Aviation Services (Democratic Republic of Congo), before being bought by Bin Mahfooz Aviation in December 1998. Bin Mahfooz Aviation is a small charter airline founded in 1992, operating out of Banjul International Airport, Gambia. This aircraft crashed during landing at Addis Ababa on 19 June 2005.

VT-DXT, Boeing 707-329C of Air India, arriving at a busy Schiphol Airport, Amsterdam, on 18 July 1970. This 707 first flew on 6 August 1968, and was delivered to Air India on 19 August 1968, serving with the airline for 19 years, until March 1987. It was sold to the Indian Air Force, as K2899, and was converted to an ELINT (Electronic Intelligence) 707-337C-H. Air India was established in 1946, and the airline's first international flight took place on 8 June 1948, when a Lockheed Constellation flew from Bombay to London Heathrow, via Basra, Cairo and Geneva.

10+02, Boeing 707-307C of the Luftwaffe, at Cologne Bonn Airport on 25 August 1991. The Luftwaffe ordered four Boeing 707-307Cs, and they were delivered during September and November 1968, based at Cologne Bonn Airport, and mainly used for VIP and cargo flights. 10+01 was stored at Hamburg in January 1997, bought by NATO, as LX-N19997, in April 1998, and then stored at Davis-Monthan AFB. 10+02 was bought by Northrop Grumman Corporation in April 1999, and converted to an E-8B, as 99-0006, for the USAF. 10+03 was sold, as 3D-SGF, to Air Gulf Falcon in November 2000 and later re-registered as ST-AQI, then 5Y-BRV. It was withdrawn from use at Sharjah Airport, United Arab Emirates, in 2005. 10+04 was stored at Hamburg in November 1996, then bought by NATO, as LX-N20000, and stored at Manching Air Base, Ingolstadt, in 2011.

FAB 2403, Boeing KC-137E of the Brazilian Air Force, at Schiphol Airport, Amsterdam, on 14 December 1999. First flown by Boeing as N707N on 15 August 1968, this aircraft was sold to VARIG on 14 July 1969 as PP-VJH. It remained in service with VARIG until 13 February 1986, when it was bought by the Força Aérea Brasileira (Brazilian Air Force), as FAB 2403, and used for transport and aerial refuelling. It was later stored at Rio de Janeiro, and was scrapped in January 2014.

CC-CEI, Boeing 707-321B of Lan-Chile, at Rio de Janeiro Airport on 23 October 1988. Chile's national flag-carrier was originally formed on 5 March 1929 as Linea Aeropostal Santiago-Arica, under the command of the Chilean Air Force. It became an autonomous company in 1932, when the Lan-Chile (Línea Aérea Nacional de Chile) title was adopted. Lan-Chile received its first Boeing 707 in April 1977, as CC-CEA, and began international services to North America and Europe. Delivered to Pan Am in December 1968 as N881PA, this 707 was bought by Lan-Chile on 7 December 1978 as CC-CEI *Valle del Elqui*. The aircraft was being towed into a hangar at Santiago Airport, on 23 June 1990, when one of the engines struck a tow truck, causing the pylon and engine to break off, which resulted in severe damage. It was broken up in 1997.

YR-JCB, Boeing 707-321B in Jaro/Aero Asia livery, at Sharjah Airport, United Arab Emirates, in January 1998. Originally delivered to Pan American World Airways on 18 December 1968, this aircraft was sold to Global International Airways in April 1983, and leased to Ladeco Airlines (Chile) in March 1989, as CC-CYB, before returning to Global in December 1994. It was then leased to Romanian carrier Jaro International in March 1995, and sub-leased to Aero Asia, as YR-JCB, for four months (hence the dual livery in the photograph). It was leased to Jordan Aviation, as JY-JAA, in April 2001, then to Sky Aviation as 3D-JAA. Kinshasa Airways bought the aircraft, as 9Q-CWK, in September 2004.

N887PA, Boeing 707-321B of Pan Am, pictured at London Stansted Airport on 21 May 1982. First flown by Boeing on 22 January 1969, this aircraft was delivered to Pan American World Airways on 31 January 1968, as N887PA *Clipper Flora Temple*, and left the Pan Am fleet in December 1980. It was then leased to Global International Airways, which bought the 707 in May 1984. It was sold to Boeing in September 1985, as N160GL, and was used for the KC-135 programme. It was stored at Davis-Monthan AFB and broken up during 2003. Pan American was formed in 1927, and opened a mail service across the Pacific in 1935, using flying boats. The first 707s went into service with Pan Am in November and December 1958.

SX-DBF, Boeing 707-384B of Olympic Airways, taking off from Hellinikon Airport, Athens, on 6 April 1973. Delivered to Olympic Airways on 23 January 1969 as SX-DBF *City of Mycenae*, this 707 left the Olympic fleet after 21 years of service and was sold to Israel Aircraft Industries in March 1990. Omega Air then bought the aircraft, as N7185T, and sold it to Boeing on 24 July 1990. It was withdrawn from use at Davis-Monthan AFB, and was used for the KC-135 programme.

P4-YYY, Boeing 707-331C MAS (Morgan Air Service) Airlines, pictured at Ostend Airport, on 2 May 1997. First flown on 30 June 1969, and delivered to Trans World Airlines on 16 July 1969, as N15713, this 707 was sold to Global International Airways in August 1978. It was operated by several leasing companies and airlines, including Race Aviation, Fast Air Chile, Aviation Leasing, Golden Horn Aviation, Buffalo Airways, Skyjet Brasil, MAS Airlines, and was bought by First International Airways in September 1997 as 9G-FIA. It was then stored at Sharjah Airport, United Arab Emirates, in 2004, and broken up in January 2006.

PT-TCN, Boeing 707- 323C operated by Trans Brasil Cargo, seen at Galeao Airport, Rio de Janeiro, on 23 October 1988. Delivered to American Airlines on 17 July 1968 as N8416, this 707 was leased to American Trans Air from November 1982 to January 1983, then bought by Trans Brasil, as PT-TCN, in March 1985. It was transferred to Trans Brasil Cargo, and then sold to BETA Cargo, as PP-BRR, in January 1997. BETA changed its name to BETA Brazilian Express in November 2000. The aircraft was then stored at Guarulhos Airport, São Paulo, in August 2006, and was broken up in March 2009.

VP-WGA, Boeing 707-344C of Air Zimbabwe, at London Gatwick Airport on 2 August 1980. This aircraft was originally built for Trek Airways, as ZS-FKT, but the order was not taken up, so it was delivered to South African Airways, as ZS-SAG, in April 1969. It was leased to Air Zimbabwe, as VP-WGA, from April 1980 to March 1981, and returned to South African Airways as ZS-SAG. It was bought by Israel Aircraft Industries in October 1982 and sold to the Israeli Air Force as 4X-JYQ, code 242, then converted to ELINT (Electronic Intelligence) specification before entering storage at Tel Aviv in 2006.

9Q-CVG, Boeing 707-358C operated by ATS Airlines, seen at Ostend Airport on 30 August 1995. This 707 was ordered by El Al, as 4X-ATX, in May 1969, and remained in service with the Israeli national carrier until November 1992. It was then sold to Israel Aircraft Industries in July 1994, and was bought by Zaire-based ATS (Air Transport Service) Airlines, as 9Q-CVG, in December 1994. ATS used the aircraft until February 1996, when it was sold to Zaire Express. A year later, it was bought by Hewa Bora Airways (Democratic Republic of Congo), before being stored and then withdrawn from use at N'Djili Airport, Kinshasa, in February 1998. The aircraft was broken up in January 2001.

ST-AKW, Boeing 707-330C of AZZA Air Transport, at Sharjah Airport, United Arab Emirates, on 12 November 2000. Originally delivered to Lufthansa, as D-ABUJ *Afrika*, on 27 February 1969, this 707 was leased to Frankfurt-based Condor from March 1977 to February 1979, and then sold to the United Arab Emirates government in May 1981 as A6-DPA. It was bought by the Sudan government in May 1986, as ST-AKW, and sold five months later to Nile Safaris Aviation. It was leased to Sudan Airways and Trans Arabian Air Transport, before being sold to Sudanese cargo carrier AZZA Transport Company, in August 1994. It was then bought by Ibis Air Transport, as P4-AKW, in February 1997 and leased back to AZZA Air Transport.

ST-AKW, Boeing 707-330C operated by Nile Safaris Aviation, seen at London Stansted Airport on 13 July 1987. Nile Safaris Aviation leased this 707 to Sudan Airways, and it was later bought by AZZA Air Transport in August 1994 (see previous photograph). On 21 October 2009, the aircraft was operating on a cargo flight, under a Sudan Airways flight number, from Sharjah, United Arab Emirates, to Khartoum. During the initial climb out of Sharjah Airport, one of the cowlings fell from the number-four engine. The crew attempted to return to the airport, after reporting the loss of an engine. The aircraft went into a steep turn, rolled to the right at a high rate, sunk, and was destroyed as it impacted the ground near the airport.

D-ABUO, Boeing 707-330C of Lufthansa, seen at Nuremberg Airport in October 1978. Ordered by Lufthansa, this aircraft first flew on 1 May 1969, and was delivered on 8 May 1969 as D-ABUO *Australia*. It was leased to German Cargo from November 1978 to October 1984, before being sold to Hill Eight Corporation on 2 October 1984 as N707HE. It was then operated by several leasing companies and airlines, including Challenge Air Cargo, Aeronautical Leasing Corporation and Panama International Airways. It was bought by Challenge Air Cargo in August 1985, stored for a period at Miami, then bought by Omega Air for use as an engine test bed. It was broken up at Melbourne, Florida, in 2018.

5Y-GFH, Boeing 707-323B of Air Gulf Falcon, at Sharjah Airport, United Arab Emirates, on 14 November 2000. Delivered to American Airlines on 9 April 1969 as N8432, this 707 was bought by travel club Ports of Call, as N708PC, in October 1983. From 1986, the Ports of Call aircraft fleet was operated by a separate charter company, rebranded as Skyworld Airlines. The aircraft was sold to MEA (Middle East Airlines) on 1 January 1990, as OD-AHF, and later sold to Falcon Air Leasing as 5Y-GFH. In June 2000, it was leased to Air Gulf Falcon, and was then stored from August 2001 at Sharjah Airport.

OD-AFE, Boeing 707-3B4C of MEA (Middle East Airlines), seen at Hellinikon Airport, Athens, on 29 June 1995. Originally delivered to MEA on 28 October 1979 as OD-AFE, this 707 was leased to Nigeria Airways and Saudia between 1975 and 1980, before returning to MEA. It was sold to Luxor Air in July 1998 as SU-BMV. On 23 March 2001, Luxor Air was flying the aircraft from Jeddah, Saudi Arabia, to Monrovia, Liberia, when it suffered a landing accident at Monrovia. All 175 passengers and seven crew survived, but the 707 was written off.

EL-ZGS, Boeing 707-309C of Jet Cargo-Liberia, at Sharjah Airport, United Arab Emirates, on 14 November 1995. This 707 first flew in October 1969, and was delivered to China Airlines in November 1969 as B-1824. It remained in service with the Chinese carrier until August 1982, when it was sold to Jet Cargo-Liberia as N707ZS. It was re-registered as EL-ZGS *Maritza*, and leased to Ethiopian Cargo in 1988. It returned to Jet Cargo-Liberia in 1992, and was stored at Dubai International Airport in 1996, before being broken up in June 2007.

B-1824, Boeing 707-309C of China Airlines, at Kai Tak Airport, Hong Kong, on 24 March 1972. China Airlines is the flag carrier of Taiwan, officially the Republic of China (as opposed to the People's Republic of China). The airline was originally founded on 10 December 1959, by a group of retired Air Force personnel, to provide charter operations with two PBY-5A Catalinas. After becoming the national carrier in 1965, China Airlines expanded rapidly, with increased domestic and international services. In its early years, the airline used aircraft such as the DC-4, Caravelle and YS-11, before Boeing 707s and 727s were introduced. The first 707 to arrive was B-1824, in November 1969, and it remained in service until August 1982.

CS-TBF, Boeing 707-382B operated by TAP (Transportes Aéreos Portugueses), seen at Schiphol Airport, Amsterdam, on 16 September 1980. This aircraft was delivered to TAP on 13 February 1970, as CS-TBF, *Vasco da Gama*. TAP became TAP Air Portugal in April 1979. Buffalo Airways bought this 707 in November 1983 as N105BV. It was sold to E-Systems Incorporated in September 1985, and converted to a C-137C, 85-6974, for the USAF. It was withdrawn from use at McConnell AFB, Wichita in August 1998.

13702, Boeing 707-347C/CC-137 of the Canadian Armed Forces, seen at Schiphol Airport, Amsterdam, in May 1982. This aircraft was originally ordered by Western Airlines, as N1507W, but the order was cancelled, and it was sold to the Canadian Armed Forces (CAF) on 28 February 1970. The CC-137 was operated by 437 Squadron as 13702. It remained in service with the CAF until November 1993, when it was bought by Omega Air as HR-AMF. It was stored at Shannon Airport in 1994, then leased to Transbrasil from July 1994 to December 1996, registered as EL-AKT. It was later sold to Northrop Grumman Corporation, and converted to an E-8C, 96-0043, for the USAF.

HK-1410, Boeing 707-359B operated by Avianca, photographed at Jorge Chavez Airport, Lima, on 2 November 1977. Ordered by Colombian airline, Avianca, this 707 first flew on 15 April 1970, and was delivered on 24 April 1970 as HK-1410. It remained in service with Avianca for 21 years, and was withdrawn from service at Bogotá Airport in May 1991. It was then bought by Air Taxi International in June 1994, transferred to Enterprise Air, as N22055, and broken up at El Dorado Airport, Bogotá, in September 1994.

G-AXGX, Boeing 707-336C of BOAC, pictured at Kai Tak Airport, Hong Kong, on 24 April 1972. Originally delivered to BOAC on 25 March 1970, as G-AXGX, and transferred to British Airways in April 1974 when the airlines merged, this aircraft was bought by the Qatar government in July 1984 as A7-AAC. It was sold to Chapman Freeman, as VR-BZA, on 14 February 1995, then bought by TBN Aircraft in March 1995. Finally, the 707 was sold to Northrop Grumman Corporation for an E-8 conversion, but the conversion was not carried out. The aircraft was stored at Lake Charles Airport, Louisiana, and broken up in 2001.

G-AXXZ, Boeing 707-336B of British Airways, at London Heathrow Airport on 31 July 1980. This aircraft was delivered to BOAC on 17 April 1971, as G-AXXZ, and transferred to British Airways in 1974, when the companies merged. It was bought by TRATCO in June 1983, and leased to West Coast Airlines, as 9G-ADB, for two months. It was then sold to the Benin government, as TY-BBR, on 4 November 1983. On 13 June 1985, during the take-off roll at Sabha Airport, Libya, the captain decided to abandon the take-off. However, the crew was unable to stop the aircraft before the end of the runway, and the 707 overran, eventually coming to rest and bursting into flames. It was written off.

9Q-CLY, Boeing 707-336C operated by GKN-EMZ Mining (Zaire), seen at London Stansted Airport on 15 August 1984. Delivered to BOAC on 28 May 1971, as G-AYLT, and transferred to British Airways when the airlines merged, this 707 has a remarkable history, as it has been operated by a considerable number of airlines over the years, including ZAS, Air Hong Kong, Gemini, Phoenix, Transasian, Simba, Air Gulf, Sky Aviation and Spirit of Africa (as ST-AQW). It was last seen operating with Sudanese States Aviation in 2009.

TJ-CAA, Boeing 707-3H7C of Cameroon Airlines, at Paris Orly Airport on 18 June 1979. Ordered by Cameroon Airlines on 20 November 1972 as TJ-CAA, this 707 was sold to Israel Aircraft Industries, as 4X-BYR, on 20 June 1987, and re-registered as 4X-JYB, code 255, for the Israeli Air Force. It was withdrawn from use in 2008. Cameroon Airlines was established on 26 July 1971, following the Cameroon government's decision to withdraw its support from the Air Afrique consortium, as of 2 September 1971. Cameroon Airlines started operations on 1 November 1971 from Douala Airport. This was the only 707 in service with the airline, arriving in 1972 for use on international services.

5N-ABK, Boeing 707-3F9C of Nigeria Airways, at Ostend Airport on 12 April 1994. This 707 was delivered to Nigeria Airways on 16 January 1973. Nigeria Airways was government-owned, and was formed in 1958 as WAAC Nigeria, to take over from West African Airways Corporation (WAAC), which dated back to 1946. The new airline began operations on 1 October 1958, and the name Nigeria Airways was adopted in 1971. 5N-ABK was used for Nigeria Airways flight WT9805 on 19 December 1994, transporting cargo from Jeddah, Saudi Arabia to Kano, Nigeria, when the aircraft crashed near Kiri Kasama, Nigeria. The probable cause of the accident was a heat-generating substance that was hidden in a consignment of fabrics in the cargo compartment of the 707. It caused an explosion that seriously impaired the flight controls. The aircraft was destroyed.

B-2404, Boeing 707-3J6B of the Civil Aviation Administration of China, seen at Bole International Airport, Addis Ababa, on 24 January 1988. Originally bought by the Civil Aviation Administration of China (CAAC), and delivered on 17 September 1973 as 2404, this aircraft was registered as B-2404 in July 1974. The operator was renamed as Air China in July 1988. The 707 was bought by Israel Aircraft Industries on 26 February 1993, and was converted to a VIP aircraft for the Angola government, as D2-TPR, in February 1995. It was stored at Luanda Airport, Angola, in 2012.

5X-TRA, Boeing 707-3J6C of Triangle Airline, pictured at Schiphol Airport, Amsterdam, on 24 June 1995. Ordered by the Civil Aviation Administration of China (CAAC), this 707 made its first flight on 25 January 1974, and was delivered on 26 February 1974 as 2418. It was registered as B-2418 in July 1974, and was transferred to China Southwest Airlines in November 1983. It was then sold to Pacific Airline Support Corporation on 12 February 1995 as B-606L. Triangle Aviation bought the aircraft on 16 June 1995, as 5X-TRA, based at Entebbe International Airport, Uganda. After six months, it was placed in storage at Tel Aviv, and was broken up in 2001.

EP-IRN, Boeing 707-386C of Iran Air, at Paris Orly Airport on 14 April 1978. Built by Boeing as N1785B, this 707 first flew on 18 April 1973, and was sold to Iran Air on 1 May 1973 as EP-IRN *Pasargad*. It was leased to Iran Air Tours from November 1995 to November 1996, then returned to Iran Air. The aircraft was then stored at Mehrabad Airport, Tehran, and transferred to the Islamic Republic of Iran Air Force as 5-8307 in November 2014.

SU-AVZ, Boeing 707-366C of Air Memphis, at Beek Airport, Maastricht, on 8 July 2002. Originally delivered to Egyptair on 29 June 1973 as SU-AVZ, this aircraft remained in service with the airline until 1994. It was then bought by National Aviation (Egypt) on 2 June 1994. It was sold to Omega Air on 15 September 1995, and immediately leased to National Aviation until May 1998. Next, it was bought by Tristar Air on 16 May 1998, and leased to Air Memphis on the same day. The aircraft was damaged beyond repair at Cairo on 2 April 2004.

S2-ADU, Boeing 707-3K1C operated by South Asian Airlines, seen at Bole International Airport, Addis Ababa, on 21 April 2005. Delivered as YR-ABA to Romanian carrier TAROM (Transporturi Aeriene Române) on 21 February 1974, this 707 was leased to Nigeria Airways, Air Algerie, LOT, Birgenair, Air Afrique, Kuwait Airways and Jaro International, before returning to TAROM in August 1998. It was stored at Otopeni Airport, Bucharest, in December 2001, and then bought by South Asian Airlines on June 2004 as S2-ADU. It was sold to Mid Express Tchad in October 2008, as TT-DAX, and was then stored at N'Djamena, Chad, in 2013.

ST-AFA, Boeing 707-3J8C of Sudan Airways, at London Heathrow Airport on 31 August 1979. Ordered by Sudan Airways, this 707 first flew on 5 June 1974, and was delivered on 17 June 1974 as ST-AFA. It served with Sudan Airways for 36 years, and was then placed in storage at Khartoum Airport in August 2010. Sudan Airways is the government-owned flag-carrier, which was founded in 1946, following the signing of an agreement with the British company Airwork Ltd, for technical and management assistance. Proving flights started in 1947 with three de Havilland Doves, and the first two Boeing 707s arrived in 1974. In the background, Boeing 720-023B, OD-AFO, of MEA (Middle East Airlines) can be seen.

A-7002, Boeing 707-3M1C of the Indonesian Air Force, pictured at Ngurah Rai Airport, Bali, on 2 October 1992. This 707 was bought by Pelita Air Services, and delivered on 25 April 1974 as PK-PJQ. It was leased to Sempatie Air Transport from August 1977 to July 1979, then sold to the Indonesian Air Force in November 1982. It was then leased to Pelita Air Services for three months, and returned to the Air Force. Another lease followed in July 1989, to Garuda Indonesian Airways as PK-GAU. The aircraft returned to the Air Force in December 1989, and was stored at Baneasa Airport, Bucharest, in May 2005. It was broken up in 2018.

HZ-HM3, Boeing 707-368C operated by the Saudi Arabian government, seen at Dusseldorf Airport on 26 May 1992. Delivered to the Saudi Arabian Royal Flight, as HZ-ACK, on 27 June 1977, this aircraft was then sold to the Saudi Arabian government in July 1979 as HZ-HM3. It was bought by the Alameda Corporation in May 2003, and stored at Baneasa Airport, Bucharest. It was then registered to Omega Air in December 2005, as N707MQ, and was converted to an aerial tanker, based at San Antonio, Texas.

1001, Boeing 707-386C of the Islamic Republic of Iran, seen at Geneva Airport on 7 October 2007. Originally delivered to the Iranian government on 3 May 1978 as EP-HIM, this 707 was transferred to the Imperial Iranian Air Force, as 1001, in July 1978. The Imperial Iranian Air Force became the Islamic Republic of Iran Air Force in February 1979, following the Islamic Revolution. The aircraft was transferred again to the Iranian government in May 1986 as EP-NHY. In May 2016, the aircraft was seen stored at Mehrabad Airport, Tehran.

N70788, Boeing 707-321 operated by Bayu Indonesia Air, pictured at Schiphol Airport, Amsterdam, on 4 January 1978. Delivered to Pan American in January 1960 as N727PA, this aircraft was leased to Alaska Airlines in April 1970, and then bought by Donaldson International Airways, as G-AWZA, in November 1971. It then passed through a number of operators, including Iraqi Airways, British Midland, MAS (Malaysian Airline System), East African Airways, Kuwait Airways, Bayu and Aerotal Colombia (in September 1980, as HK-1024). On 20 December 1980, this 707 was approaching Runway 12 at El Dorado International Airport, Bogota, when it entered heavy rain and dense fog. The aircraft descended into the ground, crash-landed and caught fire. (Peter de Groot)

HK-3355X, Boeing 707-324C of Tampa (Colombia), at El Dorado Airport, Bogotá, on 21 February 1993. This aircraft was delivered to Continental Airlines in June 1965 as N17323. It remained in service with Continental until November 1971, when it was sold to Lloyd International Airways as G-AZJM. It then served with various other airlines, such as British Caledonian, Biman Bangladesh, British Midland Airways (BMA), Air Algerie and PIA (Pakistan International Airlines). It was leased to Tampa in December 1987, and was damaged beyond repair during a heavy landing at Viracopas Airport, São Paulo, on 9 October 1994.

G-BFLD, Boeing 707-338C of British Midland Airways (BMA), pictured at Rotterdam Airport, Zestienhoven, on 25 May 1982. Delivered to Qantas Airways in April 1968, as VH-EAE, and remaining in service with the Australian carrier until March 1978, this 707 was then bought by British Midland Airways (BMA) as G-BFLD. Subsequently, it was leased to several other airlines, such as DETA (Mozambique Airlines) and Air Algerie, and then passed to ATASCO Leasing. It was bought by Burlington Express, as N862BX, and then stored at Fort Worth, Texas, in November 1993. In 1994, it was sold to ADC airlines, Nigeria, as 5N-BBD. It was broken up at Manston airport in April 2001.

9V-BBA, Boeing 707-312B operated by MSA (Malaysia-Singapore Airlines), at Kai Tak Airport, Hong Kong, on 24 March 1972. This aircraft was delivered to MSA in May 1968 as 9V-BBA. MSA was established in May 1947, and the airline name was changed to Malaysia Airways in November 1963, then evolved into Malaysia-Singapore Airlines (MSA) on 30 December 1966, when it became the joint carrier for both Malaysia and Singapore. The 707 was bought by Air Lanka, as 4R-ALB, on 25 September 1979. It was sold to Guinness Peat Aviation in July 1981, and was used for spares at Shannon Airport.

S7-4HM, Boeing 707-324C of Air Seychelles, pictured at Zurich Airport in April 1988. Delivered to Continental Airlines, as N67333, on 16 May 1968, this 707 remained with Continental until April 1972, when it was bought by Varig as PP-VLL. It was leased to Air Seychelles from February 1988 to August 1989. The aircraft was then leased to Golden Horn Aviation, as TK-GHB, and in September 1991 to Angola Air Charter as D2-TON. It was placed in storage at Luanda Airport, Angola, in December 1998.

Further reading from

As Europe's leading aviation publisher, we also produce a wide range of market-leading magazines.

Visit: shop.keypublishing.com for more details

KEY.AERO — Your Aviation Destination - Visit www.Key.Aero today